Too Poor
for
Peace?

Too Poor
for
Peace?

Global Poverty, Conflict, and Security in the 21st Century

LAEL BRAINARD

DEREK CHOLLET

Editors

BROOKINGS INSTITUTION PRESS
Washington, D.C.

Library of Congress Cataloging-in-Publication data

Too poor for peace? : global poverty, conflict, and security in the 21st century / Lael
Brainard, Derek Chollet, editors.
    p. cm.
"The chapters draw from a conference at the Aspen Institute held on August 2 to
August 4, 2006, called, "The Tangled Web: The Poverty-Insecurity Nexus."
    Summary: "Investigates the complex and dynamic relationship between poverty
and insecurity, exploring possible agents for change. Brings the latest lessons and
intellectual framework to bear in an examination of African leadership, the private
sector, and American foreign aid as vehicles for improving economic conditions and
security"—Provided by publisher.
    Includes bibliographical references and index.
    ISBN-13: 978-0-8157-1375-3 (pbk. : alk. paper)
    ISBN-10: 0-8157-1375-4 (pbk. : alk. paper)
    1. Poverty—Developing countries—Congresses. 2. Political violence—Developing
countries—Congresses. 3. Economic assistance, American—Developing countries—
Congresses. 4. Public-private sector cooperation—Congresses. 5. Peace building—
Congresses. I. Brainard, Lael. II. Chollet, Derek H. III. Title.

HC59.72.P6T66   2007
339.4'6091724—dc22   2007008943

9 8 7 6 5 4 3 2 1

The paper used in this publication meets minimum requirements of the
American National Standard for Information Sciences—Permanence of Paper for
Printed Library Materials: ANSI Z39.48-1992.

Typeset in Adobe Garamond

Composition by Cynthia Stock
Silver Spring, Maryland

Printed by R. R. Donnelley
Harrisonburg, Virginia

Contents

Foreword

WHILE THE WORLD is experiencing an unprecedented period of peace among major powers, vast numbers of people are perishing in civil wars and from other ravages associated with failed states and corrupt, incompetent, if not murderous political systems. Whether sparked by natural resource scarcities, inadequate employment opportunities for growing numbers of youths, or decrepit and corrupt institutions, intrastate conflict thrives in areas of poverty, leading to a vicious and deadly cycle between poverty and insecurity. *Too Poor for Peace? Global Poverty, Conflict, and Security in the 21st Century* explores the many facets of the tangled web between poverty and insecurity, unfolding complex ties among youth demographics, natural resources and conflict, and examining the roles of leadership, private sector engagement, and transformational diplomacy as routes to security and poverty alleviation.

This volume, edited by Lael Brainard and Derek Chollet, includes chapters by Vinca LaFleur of Vinca LaFleur Communications, Susan Rice of the Brookings Institution, Edward Miguel of the University of California, Berkeley, Colin Kahl of the University of Minnesota, Anthony Nyong of the University of Jos, and most recently, the International Development Research Centre in Nairobi, Henrik Urdal of the International Peace Research Institute in Oslo, Marc Sommers of Tufts University, Robert Rotberg of Harvard University and the World Peace Foundation, Jane Nelson of Harvard University and the Brookings Institution, and Jennifer Windsor of Freedom House.

The chapters draw from a conference at the Aspen Institute held on August 2 to August 4, 2006, called, "The Tangled Web: The Poverty-Insecurity Nexus," hosted by Richard C. Blum of Blum Capital Partners, and Lael Brainard and myself of the Brookings Institution, with the support of honorary co-chairs Mary Robinson of Realizing Rights: The Ethical Globalization Initiative and Walter Isaacson of the Aspen Institute.

The quality of this book owes much to superb research, coordination, and planning from the associate director of the Brookings Blum Roundtable, Inbal Hasbani, as well as Raji Jagadeesan and Abigail Jones.

The editors wish to thank Alfred Imhoff for rapid and terrific editing, and Janet Walker and Susan Woollen of the Brookings Institution Press for their help bringing the manuscript to publication. The authors remain responsible for their chapters and their content and any errors or omissions.

This book was made possible by generous support from Dick Blum, whom we are proud to have as a Brookings trustee, with additional support from the William and Flora Hewlett Foundation.

STROBE TALBOTT
President
The Brookings Institution

Washington, D.C.
April 2007

Too Poor
for
Peace?

1

The Tangled Web:
The Poverty-Insecurity Nexus

Lael Brainard, Derek Chollet, and Vinca LaFleur

THE FIGHT AGAINST global poverty is commonly—and appropriately—framed as a moral imperative. Stark images of suffering weigh on Western consciences, as images of hungry children in Niger, AIDS orphans in Tanzania, tsunami victims in Indonesia, and refugees in Darfur are beamed into our living rooms in real time. In today's increasingly interconnected world, the "haves" cannot ignore the suffering of the "have-nots." Whether or not we choose to care, we cannot pretend that we do not see.

Yet the effort to end poverty is about much more than extending a helping hand to those in need. In a world where boundaries and borders have blurred, and where seemingly distant threats can metastasize into immediate problems, the fight against global poverty has become a fight of necessity—not simply because personal morality demands it, but because global security does as well.

Extreme poverty exhausts governing institutions, depletes resources, weakens leaders, and crushes hope—fueling a volatile mix of desperation and instability. Poor, fragile states can explode into violence or implode into collapse, imperiling their citizens, regional neighbors, and the wider world as livelihoods are crushed, investors flee, and ungoverned territories become a spawning ground for global threats like terrorism, trafficking, environmental devastation, and disease.

Yet if poverty leads to insecurity, it is also true that the destabilizing effects of conflict and demographic and environmental challenges make it harder for leaders, institutions, and outsiders to promote human development. Civil

wars may result in as many as 30 percent more people living in poverty[1]—
and research suggests that as many as one-third of civil wars ultimately
reignite.[2]

In sum, poverty is both a cause of insecurity and a consequence of it.

If the link between poverty and insecurity is apparent, the pathway toward
solutions is far from clear. What, after all, is meant by "insecurity" and "conflict"—two terms that cover a wide range of phenomena, from the fear and
want poor individuals suffer to the armed violence that can engulf entire
regions? Is conflict driven by concrete economic factors or sociopolitical
exclusion and humiliation? Should our primary concern be internal instability or the risk that destabilizing threats will be exported? Should we worry
most about individual livelihoods or the health of the state itself? Is it necessary to address insecurity before poverty can be tackled? Should U.S. policymakers characterize development assistance as an American national security
priority or frame it in moral terms?

It is hard to know which strand to grasp first to untangle the poverty-
insecurity web. But every day, 30,000 children die because they are too poor
to survive,[3] and last year saw seventeen major armed conflicts in sixteen locations.[4] Over the next four decades, the population of developing countries
will swell to nearly 8 billion—representing 86 percent of humanity.[5]
Addressing poverty—and clearly understanding its relationship to insecurity—needs to be at the forefront of the policy agenda. The world simply
cannot afford to wait.

The Doom Spiral

In recent years, world leaders and policy experts have developed a strong consensus that the fight against poverty is important to ensuring global stability.
This was the core message of the 2005 Group of Eight Summit in Glen-
eagles, Scotland, and it is the underlying rationale of the UN Millennium
Development Goals.

American policymakers have traditionally viewed security threats as involving bullets and bombs—but now even they acknowledge the link between
poverty and conflict. Former secretary of state Colin Powell notes that "the
United States cannot win the war on terrorism unless we confront the social
and political roots of poverty."[6] The 2006 National Security Strategy of the
United States makes the case for fighting poverty because "development rein-
forces diplomacy and defense, reducing long-term threats to our national
security by helping to build stable, prosperous, and peaceful societies."[7] And

the Pentagon's 2006 Quadrennial Defense Review focuses on fighting the "long war," declaring that the U.S. military has a humanitarian role in "alleviating suffering, . . . [helping] prevent disorder from spiraling into wider conflict or crisis."[8]

Such assertions have a commonsense and compelling logic. Within states, extreme poverty literally kills; hunger, malnutrition, and disease claim the lives of millions each year. Poverty-stricken states tend to have weak institutions and are often plagued by ineffective governance, rendering them unable to meet their people's basic needs for food, sanitation, health care, and education. Weak governments are often unable to adequately control their territory—leaving lawless areas and natural resources to be hijacked by predatory actors. Fragile states can become breeding grounds for criminal activity, internal strife, or terrorist networks—and often all three simultaneously.

Extreme poverty is also both a source and product of environmental degradation—for example, the deforestation of the Amazon River and Congo River basins is damaging biodiversity and contributing to global warming. And in an age of global air travel, when traffic is expected to reach 4.4 trillion passenger-kilometers flown in 2008, it is easy to see how a disease—whether avian flu, Ebola, or SARS—originating in a developing country with poor early warning and response mechanisms could quickly threaten the lives of people far beyond its borders.[9]

The arguments linking poverty and insecurity are reinforced by recent scholarly research. Mainstream opinion, in the media and elsewhere, tends to characterize civil conflict as stemming from ancient ethnic hatreds or political rivalries. Yet the groundbreaking statistical analysis by the Oxford economist Paul Collier shows that ethnic diversity is in most cases actually a safeguard against violence; the most powerful predictors of civil conflict are in fact weak economic growth, low incomes, and dependence on natural resources. In Collier's words, countries with all three risk factors "are engaged in a sort of Russian Roulette,"[10] struggling to promote development before the bullets start to fly.

It is true that war itself impoverishes, but the Berkeley economist Edward Miguel and his colleagues have helped establish convincingly that increases in poverty on their own significantly increase the likelihood of conflict. Miguel examined annual country-level data for forty-one countries in sub-Saharan Africa between 1981 and 1999 whose populations depend on subsistence agriculture, and he showed that the drop in per capita income associated with drought significantly increases the likelihood of civil conflict in the following year.[11] Given that drought is a natural phenomenon, the analysis suggests that violent conflict is driven by poor economic outcomes, and not the other way round. Conversely, this research shows that as such economic factors as personal income and national growth rates rise, the risk of conflict falls. For each additional percentage point in the growth rate of per capita income, the chances for conflict are about 1 percent less; doubling the level of income cuts the risk of conflict in half. According to the U.K. Department for International Development, a country with $250 per capita income has a 15 percent likelihood of internal conflict over five years—many times greater than the 1 percent risk to an economy with $5,000 per capita income.[12]

Why is the risk of conflict higher in poor countries? Some suggest that it is because poor people have little to lose; as *The Economist* wrote, "it is easy to give a poor man a cause."[13] In addition, governments of poor countries often have little tax base with which to build professional security forces and are vulnerable to corruption. Moreover, poverty is often associated with political exclusion, humiliation, and alienation—a poverty of dignity and voice. Finally, while the data do not confirm a causal linkage between a country's income inequality and the risk of civil war, recent trends from Mexico to India to China suggest that rising expectations that go unmet may also fuel unrest. In the words of Oxfam USA's president, Raymond Offenheiser, "It isn't just who's poor that matters, but who *cares* about being poor."

Tragically, poverty and insecurity are mutually reinforcing, leading to what the Brookings scholar Susan Rice evocatively calls a "doom spiral." Conflict increases infant mortality, creates refugees, fuels trafficking in drugs and weapons, and wipes out infrastructure. It also makes it harder for outside players to deliver assistance and less attractive for the global private sector to invest. Thus, once a country has fallen into the vortex, it is difficult for it to climb out—as the world has witnessed with the ongoing catastrophe in the Democratic Republic of Congo, a crisis that has claimed nearly 4 million lives and sparked a massive humanitarian emergency, where most people today are killed not by weapons but by easily preventable and treatable diseases.

Violent conflict also produces considerable economic spillover for neighboring countries, as refugees flow in, investment pulls out, and supply chains and trade routes are disrupted. Moreover, mass movements of people— whether armed rebels or civilian refugees—can be regionwide conveyor belts of infectious disease.

Although the overall number of internal and interstate wars is decreasing, a group of regions and countries remains vulnerable to conflicts over protracted periods—often cycling back into conflict after stability has been established. Instability is largely concentrated in and around the poorest parts of sub-Saharan Africa, and frontline states where Islamic extremists are engaged in violent conflict, such as Chechnya, Kashmir, Lebanon, Sudan, East Timor, Iraq, and Afghanistan. Unfortunately, poor economic conditions, weak governance, and natural resource barriers in these areas mean that violent conflict and displacement are likely to continue—and worsen—without intervention.

What, then, might be useful guidelines for tackling the poverty-insecurity challenge? The first is to help policymakers better understand the issue's significance and urgency. Part of that task is educating the press and public to replace the convenient narrative that "age-old" hatreds drive violence with a more sophisticated grasp of the links between economic drivers and conflict.

The second guideline is to understand the specific conditions that heighten the risk of conflict and human insecurity. These may include deteriorating health conditions, corrupt governments, and inadequate institutions. Two areas in particular that can exacerbate instability and merit special attention are environmental insecurity and large youth demographics.

Most of all, it is clear that tackling the poverty-insecurity nexus is a challenge that demands commitment. Promoting lasting stability requires building long-term local capacity. Interventions that work at one point may lose their potency over time and need to be adjusted to new circumstances. And research suggests that assistance is most effective not in the immediate aftermath of a conflict, when donor interest is typically greatest, but in the middle of the first postconflict decade, when the recipient country's absorptive capacity has improved.

Yet such long-term attention is too often hard to secure in rich-country capitals where players, parties, and administrations change, and where the "urgent" typically trumps the "important" on the policy agenda. Until global mind-sets shift from reactive to proactive, and from responsive to preventive, breaking out of the poverty-insecurity trap will remain an elusive goal.

A State of Nature: The Environmental Challenge

Natural resource scarcity and abundance have always been intertwined with poverty and insecurity. Today, throughout West Africa, poor villagers struggle with the effects of desertification, which degrades the land on which they farm. In Haiti, forest and soil loss aggravates the country's economic woes and sparks periods of conflict. In Pakistan, women walk long distances to collect drinking water from ponds that are used by livestock, leading to tremendous health challenges and high infant mortality. Resource abundance also has its perils: In eastern Congo, innocents are terrorized by rebels whose weapons were financed with looted diamonds.

When it comes to extreme poverty, the natural resource challenge is usually seen as one of scarcity—typically of such renewable resources as water, timber, and arable land that are fundamental for daily survival. Demographic and environmental stresses can exacerbate demands on already weakened states. These grievances can foment instability from below. When demand for resources outweighs supply, when the distribution is perceived to be grossly unfair, and when tensions exist over whether they should be treated as rights or commodities, public frustration can spark civil strife.

In addition, elites may be tempted to manipulate scarce resources—controlling them for personal gain, using them to reward certain groups over others, or even fueling "top-down" violence in an effort to maintain power. Scarcity is also often the result of severe imbalances of wealth, which is almost always a key factor in the outbreak of conflict in poor areas.

The challenges of resource scarcity will only intensify over time. During the next twenty years, more than 90 percent of the world's projected growth will take place in countries where the majority of the population is dependent on local renewable resources.[14] Almost 70 percent of the world's poor live in rural areas, and most depend on agriculture for their main income—which both requires and exhausts natural resources. More than 40 percent of the planet's population—2.4 billion people—still use wood, charcoal, straw, or cow dung as their main source of energy, and more than 1.2 billion people lack access to clean drinking water.[15]

Yet resource abundance poses equally dangerous challenges—generally concerning nonrenewable and more easily "lootable" mineral wealth like oil, gas, gold, or diamonds. More than fifty developing countries, home to 3.5 billion people, depend on natural resource revenues as an important source of government income, and many suffer from a poverty of plenty.[16]

This so-called resource curse leads to pathologies of authoritarian and corrupt regimes, led by elites who have few incentives to invest in social development or alleviate social inequities. Abundance can also create "rentier" states, whose resource revenues allow government officials to finance themselves without directly taxing their citizenry, enabling them to more easily restrict political and other rights in return for a measure of social welfare and stability; or leading to "honey pot effects," in which rogue groups fight to secure valuable natural resources—which, once acquired, provide additional means to buy weapons, fueling a cycle of growing instability.[17]

For example, though companies like ExxonMobil and Shell have poured money and infrastructure into the oil-rich Niger Delta, the region suffers from sustained conflict and instability. Nigeria currently earns $3 billion a month from oil exports, yet the Delta remains deeply poor. Militant groups, tapping into local frustration at the continued deep poverty in this oil-rich region awash with oil revenues, have fueled violence. Local attacks continue each day, growing more sophisticated and organized, making one of the world's most resource-rich areas also one of its most dangerous.[18]

What, then, are some of the measures states and outside actors can take to attenuate the risks that resource scarcity and dependence pose to human security?

The place to begin is with sensible government policies that promote economic diversification, capacity building, equitable distribution, enforceable property rights, demographic sustainability, and public health. In addition, countries should be encouraged to explore innovative opportunities to benefit from their renewable resources, as Brazil has done by transforming its sugarcane into ethanol, and PlayPumps International and WaterAid continue to do in Africa by providing safe drinking water to local citizens (as described in box 1-1). Outside actors, including nongovernmental organizations (NGOs), can play an important role in defusing disinformation and rumors about who is benefiting from limited natural resources, because such misunderstandings sometimes create more problems than resource scarcity itself.

Meanwhile, governments, NGOs, and private actors need to be more creative in devising tailored, targeted, emergency assistance for states facing sudden economic and environmental catastrophes. For example, foreign assistance could be quickly and routinely deployed to states that suffer a drought or commodity price collapse, *before* violence has a chance to break out. In addition, crop insurance programs and other forms of protection could be created for individuals whose livelihoods may be destroyed.[19]

Just as critical, especially in cases of natural resource abundance, are efforts to promote transparency—not only on the budget side of the ledger, but on the expenditure side as well. Publicizing how much money is flowing in for natural resources, and how it is being allocated, makes it harder for governments to skim from the top, and for rebels to benefit from plunder. According to the Publish What You Pay campaign, by 2003, U.S. investment in African oil exceeded $10 billion per year, representing two-thirds to three-quarters of the total annual U.S. investment on the continent. If the revenues

---

BOX 1-1
Not a Drop to Drink?

An acute resource problem besets one of life's most basic necessities: water. As Anthony Nyong, associate professor at the University of Jos, argues, "Many countries are moving from water stress to water scarcity to water-driven conflict." According to the World Health Organization, more than 5 million people die every year from contaminated water or water-related diseases (Peter H. Gleick, "Dirty Water: Estimated Deaths from Water-Related Diseases 2000–2020," Research Report, Pacific Institute, 2002, 4). "Many of the wars of the 20th century were about oil, but wars of the 21st century will be over water," explains Ismail Serageldin, a former vice president of the World Bank (Jason J. Morrissette and Douglas A. Borer, "Where Oil and Water Do Mix: Environmental Scarcity and Future Conflict in the Middle East and North Africa," *Parameters,* Winter 2004–5, 86–101; the citation here is on p. 86). Some observers predict that the Nile River basin could be a major site of future conflicts, with 200 million people and many African countries dependent on its flow.

Some practical solutions are emerging. WaterAid, an NGO dedicated to alleviating poverty and disease caused by unsafe water and sanitation, has joined forces with Cadbury Schweppes and Kuapa Kokoo (a farmers' cooperative that is part of the Fairtrade system) to improve the lives of cocoa farmers in Ghana by building water wells across the region. More than 300 wells have been constructed since the launch of the program in 2000,

---

from such investments were transparently and accountably managed, they could provide the basis for economic growth and poverty reduction.[20] As discussed in box 1-2, some practical programs are emerging that tackle this crucial challenge.

But such initiatives, promising as they are, are the exception rather than the rule. And important new challenges are looming—for example, China's emergence as a powerful new player in the energy and commodity sectors may have serious worldwide ramifications as Chinese investors demonstrate a willingness to make deals with unsavory regimes that have little regard for social and environmental consequences. As Harvard University and Brookings Institution scholar Jane Nelson writes, "These new players don't face the revolutionizing life for the communities by providing clean and safe drinking water and improving farming practices. Even more, the wells have freed up time for children to go to school and focus on schoolwork, instead of spending long hours fetching water for their families (for more information, see www.cadburyschweppes.com/EN/EnvironmentSociety/CaseStudies/Building Wells.htm).

Another innovative, multisector initiative is PlayPumps International, which provides uniquely sustainable water pumps across South Africa powered by the force of children playing. PlayPumps work as children spin on a merry-go-round, pumping water from underground into an easily accessible tank nearby. When they are installed near schools, PlayPumps give women and children access to safe drinking water with a simple tap. Nearly 700 PlayPumps systems have been installed in South Africa, improving the lives of more than a million people, and a recent multisector investment in PlayPumps by the U.S. government, the Case Foundation, and the MCJ Foundation means that even more children and women will benefit from PlayPumps for years to come (for more information, see www.playpumps.org).

The opportunities to act are within reach, but time is not on our side. According to a Pacific Institute analysis, between 34 and 76 million people could perish because of water-related diseases by 2020, even if the UN Millennium Development Goals are met (Gleick, "Dirty Water," 1).

same civic activism, reputation threats, and legal challenges in their home countries as do their Western counterparts when it comes to accusations of labor, human rights, and environmental abuses."[21] The time is now to start encouraging Chinese business executives to play a responsible role in promoting resource transparency and accountability in the countries where they invest. Leaders from business, government, and civil society in the West should engage in a series of frank dialogues with their Chinese counterparts to share the hard-won lessons that have ultimately led many business leaders to embrace social and environmental standards and resource transparency as serving their own core business interests no less than the communities in which they operate.

BOX 1-2
Powering Growth: The Road to Resource Transparency

Recent years have witnessed pathbreaking efforts to hold governments and corporations accountable for natural resource transactions. In June 2002, the Publish What You Pay campaign was founded to help local citizens hold their leaders accountable for the responsible management of oil, gas, and mining revenues by encouraging oil and mining companies to disclose their payments to developing country governments. Also in 2002, the British government launched the Extractive Industries Transparency Initiative. As of 2006, more than twenty producing countries from Nigeria to Azerbaijan to Peru are following industry's lead, linking, as Prime Minister Tony Blair put it, "Publish What You Pay with Publish What You Earn" (Tony Blair, "Extractive Industries Transparency Initiative," opening remarks at the London Conference on Extractive Industries Transparency Initiative, June 17, 2003, 4).

In 2002, the Open Society Institute created Revenue Watch programs in resource-rich countries to equip civil society, the media, and the public with the tools to monitor their government's use of natural resource revenues and to train policymakers to manage these revenues wisely. At the Brookings Institution, David de Ferranti developed the Transparency and Accountability Project in the spring of 2006 to strengthen the capacity of domestic civil society organizations (CSOs) to provide substantive analysis of budget choices and the distribution of public spending. The goal is for CSOs to become effective and sustainable mechanisms for holding governments accountable, leading to the more efficient and effective use of scarce public resources, and ultimately, better development outcomes.

Visionary programs like these have helped to heighten global public awareness of natural resource transactions, but the effort must continue. Natural resource revenues have the power to fuel economic development in impoverished countries, but only if such revenues are responsibly managed, allocated, and delivered.

Finally, transcending questions of natural resource scarcity or abundance within individual states are major transnational environmental challenges—such as global climate change. Population growth, deforestation, and industrialization in developing countries are accelerating the global warming process that is already under way. Rising surface temperatures on the Earth could fuel extreme weather; melting polar ice caps could cause severe flooding; shrinking glaciers could result in perilous water shortages; and continued climate change could irreversibly damage the Earth's ecosystem—even driving some species into extinction. In addition, rising temperatures could spur the spread of dangerous diseases, from malaria to dengue fever.

The brunt of climate change is likely to hit developing countries hardest, because their economies are more dependent on agriculture, their resources for coping are more limited, and because many have sizable populations in areas that could be devastated by flooding. Both rich and poor nations must join in dealing with this shared strategic threat—and develop a collective sense of urgency and commitment—before it is too late.

An Age of Youth: The Demographic Challenge

As the United States braces itself for retiring baby boomers, and European welfare states struggle to support their aging populations, the developing world is getting younger. Nearly half the people on the planet are under twenty-five years old, and more than a billion people are between the ages of ten and nineteen.[22] The disproportionately large share of young people in the population—the so-called youth bulge—is in absolute and relative terms the largest cohort ever to transition into adulthood, and it will remain so over the next two decades.

This fact presents tremendous challenges, particularly for the developing world. Young people often suffer the most from poverty, lack of educational and economic opportunities, poor health, crime, and armed conflict. Nearly 17 million of the world's youth are refugees or internally displaced persons,[23] 130 million are illiterate,[24] as many as 300,000 fight as child soldiers,[25] and collectively, young people make up almost 60 percent of the world's poor.[26]

Moreover, there is strong historical evidence linking youth bulges to instability and conflict. Henrik Urdal of the International Peace Research Institute in Oslo looked into conflicts dating back to 1946 to determine whether youth bulges increase the risk of conflict significantly. Using rigorous statistical analysis, he determined that for each percentage point increase in youth population as a share of the adult population, the risk of conflict increases by more than 4 percent. Furthermore, he argues that "when youth make up more than 35 percent of the adult population, which they do in many developing countries, the risk of armed conflict is 150 percent higher than in countries with an age structure similar to most developed countries."[27]

Paul Collier adds to this assertion by noting that the mere existence of a large youth demographic lowers the cost of recruitment for rebel armies.[28] Jack Goldstone of George Mason University observes that rising youth bulges coupled with rapid urbanization have been important contributors to political violence, particularly in the context of unemployment and poverty.[29] Taken together, the research seems to suggest a clear relationship between youth bulges and an increased risk of conflict.

The problem may lie in the fact that in too many places, the next generation is caught in a troubling cycle where the opportunities to make a useful contribution to society diminish as the number of youth soars. Yet, this need not—and, in terms of economic theory, ought not—be the case. A youthful population can be a country's blessing instead of its curse, providing a "demographic dividend" of energetic workers to jump-start productivity and growth.

The problem is that a country hoping to achieve such a positive outcome must provide economic opportunities for its young people—and too often, those reaching adulthood face bleak prospects of employment. Saudi Arabia, for example, will have 4 million young people joining the labor force in this decade—a number equivalent to two-thirds of the current Saudi workforce.[30] And when these young people have had their expectations raised through education, their frustration at not being able to earn a living can render them susceptible to extremists. As Tufts University professor Mark Sommers writes, "It often seems that nations don't know what to do with their own young people, while armed groups keep discovering new ways to make use of them."[31]

Too often, assistance programs intended to make a difference for youth are driven more by donor priorities and preconceptions than by what young people themselves really need; for example, too many job programs are designed to lure urban migrants back to the land, instead of accepting that many urbanized youth do not want to leave the city.

The problem is compounded by policy inefficiencies at the national and multinational levels—including the lack of political priority attached to youth issues; the absence of an integrated approach involving not only youth ministries but also health, education, labor, and culture; the lack of empirical data on what works; and the mismatch between money spent on education and money spent on ensuring that jobs are available when young people graduate—through programs supporting entrepreneurship, job creation, and enterprise development.

In certain places and policy circles, the result has been that young people, especially males, are seen only as menaces to their communities. They are often depicted negatively, as problems to be dealt with rather than potential to be tapped; and more is made of the fact that men are disproportionately responsible for violent crime than of the fact that the vast majority of young men, even those in brutally harsh and desperate conditions, never resort to violence.

The challenge, then, in crafting an effective response to the "youth bulge" is to resist the temptation to view young people solely as a threat—and instead approach them as a valuable resource to be protected and cultivated. Indeed, as those who work with disadvantaged youth will readily argue, there is much to be learned from the incredible resilience and resourcefulness of poor young people.

Increasingly, the international community is rising to the challenge. Of the UN's eight Millennium Development Goals, seven relate directly or indirectly to the plight of young people. In addition, the World Bank's *World Development Report 2007* addresses "development and the next generation," which should spark further analysis and better focus assistance programs.

Innovative private sector players and NGOs are also working to engage and empower youth in underprivileged areas. For example, in 2006 the ImagineNations group received support from the Bill and Melinda Gates Foundation to develop programs that provide training and capital to a new generation of young entrepreneurs. The goal is not only to spur investments in small and medium-sized enterprises but also to create incentives for larger companies to hire young people or recruit them as interns and apprentices. And the Brookings Institution's Wolfensohn Center for Development recently launched a new program—described in box 1-3—that creates new opportunities for youth in the Middle East who suffer from economic, social, and political exclusion.

Another promising initiative is Youth Business International (YBI), an international network of programs created through the Prince's Trust in the United Kingdom to help disadvantaged young people become entrepreneurs. According to YBI director Andrew Fiddaman, "There are 300 million young people aged eighteen to thirty who are un- or underemployed. Twenty percent have the potential to start a business, but only 5 percent do." YBI provides business mentoring and seed funding of between $500 and $10,000. Typically, the young entrepreneurs repay the YBI loan within three years. More than 13,000 businesses have been created through YBI, with a more than 70 percent survival rate; and as each new enterprise takes firm root, another young leader learns how to build a business, develop a credit history, and ultimately become an employer himself or herself.[32]

Other organizations are pursuing grassroots efforts to make youth an integral part of community safety and well-being. In Liberia, a local organization

BOX 1-3
From Exclusion to Inclusion: Engaging Youth in the Middle East

The Middle East has before it what could be one of the greatest demographic gifts in modern history—a potential economic windfall arising from a young and economically active workforce. Today, young people aged fifteen to twenty-four years account for 22 percent of the region's total population, the highest regional average worldwide. With the right mix of policies, this demographic opportunity could be tapped to spur economic growth and promote stability.

Yet millions of young people are already growing up in the Middle East without significant economic prospects. Youth unemployment in the region stands at 25 percent, the highest level in the world. In many Middle Eastern countries, unemployment is at its heart a youth problem; in Syria, for example, youth account for 80 percent of the unemployed.

The Brookings Institution's Wolfensohn Center for Development recently launched an initiative focusing on youth exclusion in Egypt, Iran, Syria, and Morocco. The initiative spotlights two main youth transitions to adulthood—the transition from education to employment, and the transition to household formation through marriage and family. Through an alliance of academics, policymakers, the private sector, and civil society, the Wolfensohn Center will help craft more effective policies to create opportunities for young people in the region.

While many Middle Eastern youth might enjoy higher levels of education compared with their peers in South Asia, Latin America, or Africa, the majority of them still lack employment opportunities that meet their rising expectations. This second-generation development challenge—where high levels of poverty are replaced by widespread exclusion from economic, social, and political life—confronts almost every country in the region. How the Middle East tackles this challenge will offer valuable lessons far beyond its borders.

called Youth Crime Watch Liberia is working to assist schools and communities in establishing and sustaining crime prevention programs, including a rape awareness campaign; and in Kibera, one of Nairobi's poorest slums, Carolina for Kibera, a grassroots NGO founded by a former U.S. marine, Rye Barcott, launched a youth recycling program called Trash for Cash, through which young people not only clean up their communities but also earn incomes.

As additional programs and policies are developed, several issues should be kept in mind. The first is the overarching obligation to ensure that youth efforts cut across many sectors. Governments need help developing effective, constructive, comprehensive national youth policies—and that depends in part on getting a better grip on what actually works and what does not.

The world also needs a concerted effort to provide employment opportunities for young people in poor countries—and this is an area where the private sector has a critical role to play, especially by ensuring that training and skill development are linked to market demands.

At the same time, policymakers must remember that poor youth, especially those in conflict situations, too often find themselves marginalized from political discussions and processes. Thus, as leaders and activists think about providing opportunities for educated youth, they must think not only in economic terms but political terms as well.

Special attention should also be paid to postconflict environments and efforts to help youth lift themselves out of poverty. Too often, assistance efforts focus on the most urgent priorities of postconflict situations—reducing the numbers of weapons and soldiers—at the cost of programs to address the long-term future of combatants, many if not most of whom are young. As Jane Holl Lute, the assistant secretary general of UN peacekeeping operations, notes, "DDR" programs that disarm and demobilize fighters are useless without funding and a strategy for the "R"—the crucial process of reintegration into society.

Policymakers should position programs in the cities and places where youth actually are; and they should use new media to reach young people in meaningful ways. Youth should be encouraged and trusted to organize, lead, or govern programs as much as possible. There may be useful lessons to be learned from religious groups and even fundamentalist organizations that have proven good at mobilizing and motivating poor youth. And, crucially, the world community must also invest in letting kids be kids—with funding for programs such as recreation, leisure, sport, and the arts.

Agents of Change

The challenges that can hasten insecurity in poverty-stricken environments are both complex and dynamic. Though environmental and demographic factors may serve as imminent warning signs, they by no means represent an exhaustive list of the potential causes of conflict. As we know all too well, such factors as the spread of HIV/AIDS, rapid urbanization, and fledgling institutions—among a host of other issues—may also exacerbate the risks leading to insecurity.

Such a wide array of challenges begs the question, "Where do we begin?" Regardless of whether change originates in governmental institutions, the private sector, or civil society, one constant is that leadership matters.

The Role of Leaders: Spotlight on Africa

Countries on every continent suffer from poverty and insecurity, in part because of their political leaders' decisions and actions—and no country is immune from hapless, corrupt, or even venal leadership, as citizens from the Americas to Europe to Asia would readily volunteer. And yet, some regions with weak institutions have been more deeply afflicted by poor leadership than others. Postcolonial Africa in particular has borne the burdens of a leadership deficit.

It is true that African countries have several inherent disadvantages to overcome. Their independence from outside rule is relatively recent; the United States, after all, has been engaged in its democratic experiment for more than two centuries. Africa is the world's second most populous continent, comprising fifty-three countries—fifteen of which are landlocked and many of which are tropical. At the same time, many African countries possess great human and natural resources. And yet, according to Harvard University scholar Robert Rotberg, by some measures, 90 percent of sub-Saharan African nations have experienced despotic rule in the past three decades.[33]

Poor leadership can take a devastating toll on human security. In Zimbabwe, for example, Robert Mugabe has transformed a regional economic and political success story into a repressive, chaotic mess. Fifteen years ago, a quarter of Zimbabweans were unemployed; today, the figure is 70 percent, and inflation has climbed to more than 1,000 percent a year. Meanwhile, newspapers have been closed and scores of reporters thrown in jail, while Zimbabwe's police and armed forces have forcibly eradicated slum dwellers in ways reminiscent of the horrific ethnic cleansing witnessed during the 1990s in the Balkans.[34]

Human agency is to blame for millions of civilian deaths in Africa in recent years from Congo to Sudan, Angola, Rwanda, and Darfur. Moreover, the "half-life" of damage done by bad leaders can far transcend the period of misrule. Perceptions matter, especially when countries try to attract foreign investment from half a world away, and a country that has been associated with instability or corruption in the past may find its public image hard to repair for years or even decades to come.

Polling data confirm that Africans desire honest leaders and effective governments. And the experience of countries like Botswana shows that such aspirations can indeed be achieved. Blessed with a strong tradition of open discussion, a cultural heritage that values collective wisdom and accountability, and, significantly, diamond wealth, Botswana had key resources to draw on in building a strong democracy. Yet, Botswana's success cannot be divorced from the leadership its presidents have provided. In the forty years since independence, Seretse Khama, Ketumile Masire, and Festus Mogae have used not only government tools but also their personal example to transform Botswana from a poor pastoral country into one of the continent's wealthiest and most stable—distributing the benefits of diamonds broadly, including the provision of free universal education and health care.[35] Today, President Mogae is providing a model for other African leaders to emulate in his proactive and tireless crusade against the HIV/AIDS pandemic.

Likewise, Mauritius—once a poor sugar colony—today boasts one of Africa's strongest economies, thanks to creative, honest leadership, market opening, and a political arena characterized by coalition building. During the past two decades, per capita income in Mauritius has nearly doubled, with an attendant rise in human development indicators.[36] And Mozambique, which suffered nearly two decades of civil war, has since 1997 achieved average annual growth in gross domestic product of 8.9 percent, increased enrollment in primary schools by 25 percent, and reduced extreme poverty—even as it has built one of Southern Africa's more stable new democracies.[37]

Enlightened leaders with vision and strength are especially important where the state's organizational and institutional capacity to govern is lacking. Unsurprisingly, states that successfully manage to provide their citizens with basic security, political freedom, transportation and communication infrastructure, medical necessities, and educational institutions—states like Botswana, Mauritius, and South Africa—possess the most farsighted and effective leadership.

African leadership must come from within, but outsiders can help. For the international community, the challenge is to help find, train, and support the leaders of tomorrow—and assist those who are making a difference today. The United States has a strong tradition of identifying and mentoring leadership, through the Truman Scholarship, the White House Fellows Program, the Presidential Management Fellowship, and many other initiatives; other rich countries do as well. Yet many African leaders have risen to power from

the vanguard of military or protest groups rather than an executive management background. Developing leadership mentoring programs for talented
Africans in the twenty- to forty-year-old age bracket—not only within their
respective countries but on a regional basis as well—could help a new generation of leaders hone the skills, form the networks, and internalize the ethos of
public service that would serve them and their homelands in the future.

Another promising approach is to provide what the Open Society Institute and the United Nations Development Program call a "capacity-building
fund" to supplement the incomes of effective public servants in poor countries—and thereby encourage expatriates and others who have many other
alternatives to devote their considerable expertise to the challenge of governing in their homelands. Such funds have helped support a living wage for
government officials from Serbia to Georgia to Nigeria—but they are neither
intended nor designed to be a long-term solution.

Innovative thinkers have also proposed examining the "last stop" on the
leadership journey—not just where leaders come from or what they do while
in office but also where they go once they leave. In most Western countries,
former heads of state are granted lifelong privileges—from status and security
to significant moneymaking opportunities in the private sector. In poor
countries, however, the prospect of life beyond leadership may be unappeal-
ing, especially to a president who has grown attached and accustomed to the
perks of office. Box 1-4 describes an exciting new program that encourages
leaders to transition out of government, while helping them envision a desirable future once they step down.

The international community has other tools to encourage good governance and accountability, for example, the incentive-based approach of the
U.S. Millennium Challenge Corporation (MCC). By providing aid to countries with a proven commitment to reducing poverty and strengthening
democracy, the MCC seeks to reward leaders that rule justly, invest in their
people, and encourage economic freedom. The MCC does not aspire to be
the only tool in the development kit—but it does provide substantial
amounts of assistance to countries that can meet its criteria.[38]

At the same time, honest observers acknowledge not only the difficulty of
cultivating effective leadership from the outside but also the ways in which
outside actors may contribute to the leadership problem. Strategic and diplomatic demands have prevented the United States and other Western governments from being consistent in their criticism of African and other developing country leaders around the world—and the lion's share of U.S. assistance

BOX 1-4
Rewarding Good Governance

Retirement is often considered the prize at the end of a long career. But in Africa, retiring from office generally means leaving a well-paid position with extensive perks for limited and unattractive opportunities. Responding to the lack of incentives available to retiring African leaders, Mohamed Ibrahim, the Sudanese founder of Celtel International, launched a $5 million annual prize in October 2006 to entice leaders to exit office (see www. moibrahimfoundation.org/index.html). The annual prize, awarded based on a complex index devised by Robert Rotberg of Harvard University's John F. Kennedy School of Government, will go to that sub-Saharan African leader who has demonstrated the greatest commitment to democracy and good governance during his or her tenure.

Although African leaders have tried to institute collective mechanisms to promote better leadership and more democratic governance in the past, corrupt and ruthless leaders still stand. Partnerships such as the African Leadership Council and the New Partnership for Africa's Development (NEPAD) demonstrate a commitment to improving governance, but so far the results have been mixed. For example, though NEPAD created the African Peer Review Mechanism to monitor and identify governance weaknesses, it has so far failed a critical test by proving reluctant to condemn President Mugabe's record in Zimbabwe.

Ibrahim's annual prize adds a new dynamic to the equation. By offering a financial incentive to break the pattern of long, uninterrupted, and indefinite tenure by often increasingly unaccountable leaders, the prize actively encourages leaders to rule democratically—and then hand over the reins of power at the end of their legal terms. Limited-term appointments and peaceful transfers of power are at the very heart of democratic and effective government; they inject fresh energy and ideas into the policy arena and give citizens a reliable process for holding leaders accountable. Innovative programs like Ibrahim's prize—combined with systematic efforts to strengthen civil society and create accountable and transparent institutions—are the type of bold action required to help transform African governance.

flows to countries based on their strategic importance, with the net result that U.S. assistance on a per capita basis actually declines as governance improves. And despite the West's professed desire to support development in Africa and elsewhere, trade policies and agricultural subsidies are undermining many poor countries' best hope for economic growth—thereby shackling the ability of democratically elected leaders to deliver results to their people.

Leadership from the Private Sector and the Nongovernmental Community

Although good governance and capable public institutions are indispensable, the fight against extreme poverty can only be won with active leadership from the private sector and civil society.

The global private sector has many avenues to engage in this vital effort. Investing in poverty-plagued areas offers tremendous opportunities to enhance both market value and social value; moreover, the private sector can bring to the fight against global poverty the same spirit of leadership, innovation, and initiative—and the same skills in scaling size up, driving costs down, and reaching out to new clients—required for success in the global marketplace. And in contrast to the slow and uncertain pace of public sector action on budget appropriations or the adoption of reforms, the private sector has the power to take meaningful steps against poverty right away.

Sometimes, the core business activity of an enterprise makes the development difference—for example, a mobile telephone service provider, a microfinance institution, or a utility company. In other cases, the peace and prosperity dividend comes more from the corporation's role and example in the community where it operates. As former UN secretary general Kofi Annan has explained, private sector decisions "on investment and employment, on relations with local communities, on protection for local environments, [and] on their own security arrangements, can help a country turn its back on conflict, or exacerbate the tensions that fueled the conflict in the first place."[39]

Michael Stewart of McKinsey & Company confirms that contemporary discussions on corporate social responsibility among client companies have greatly evolved; today, there is far more awareness that multinationals' business models can influence the prospects for local stability and that core business interests are directly tied to the stability and prosperity of the communities where they work. Though corporate chiefs might once have dismissed transparency as a government issue, there is growing recognition that the diversion of tax and royalty payments by local government officials can damage business directly by tarnishing reputations, and indirectly, by undermining local conditions. Managing risks and maximizing profits cannot come at the cost of exacerbating social problems or fueling conflict—and corporate executives are focusing more intensively on the need for collective, proactive, strategic action and business statesmanship.

Jane Nelson has described three basic categories of management challenges and opportunities for corporations—and also NGOs—doing business in countries plagued by political, economic, or physical insecurity.

First and foremost is an organization's obligation to do no harm—to ensure that the enterprise itself does not spark or exacerbate insecurity or conflict. As Nelson explains, while the media spotlight in recent years has been trained on resource extraction industries, other sectors also face challenges—for example, food and beverage companies that may strain limited water resources; manufacturing companies that may lower the bar on workplace safety for poor laborers; or tourism companies that may pose risks to local environments and vulnerable cultures.

New accountability mechanisms have been established in recent years to help corporations manage the "do no harm" imperative—including a wide array of global codes, compacts, and voluntary principles focused on integrating performance standards and accountability into the work of companies and NGOs, from the UN Global Compact to the banking sector's Equator Principles and the diamond industry's Kimberley Process. A growing number of global corporations are seeking to adhere to corporate social responsibility approaches that set standards for best practices and establish basic principles for operating in poor and insecure environments.

The second category of engagement is investing in local socioeconomic development and community resilience—by increasing economic opportunity and inclusion; providing access to credit and insurance; enhancing communications and technology infrastructure; and supplying basic resources to improve living conditions. Recent years have witnessed a welcome burst of new activity in these areas, driven by creative social entrepreneurs; innovative, socially conscious investors; and bold partnerships among multinational corporations, philanthropic institutions, government agencies, and others. Such innovative work has not gone unnoticed. In 2006, Muhammad Yunus won the Nobel Peace Prize for his pathbreaking efforts to provide credit to the poor in rural Bangladesh. Today, the Grameen Bank, which Yunus founded in 1976, has over 6 million borrowers, 97 percent of whom are women.

There is also a growing awareness that companies and NGOs can and should play a larger role in supporting civil society organizations, the media, and such high-risk groups as youth, women, and ethnic minorities. By helping to build more effective community advocates for good governance and security, whether through philanthropy or local investment, the private sector can help develop greater opportunities while promoting high returns. And by choosing to operate in a way that focuses on addressing the grievances and needs of traditionally disenfranchised groups like women and youth, the private sector can help enhance long-term stability. As Robert Annibale, the global director of Citigroup Microfinance, explains, "We've transformed the way we think about civil society. We recognize now that civil society includes our clients, our customers, our employees. This perspective has led us to be more consultative in our approach."

The third level of engagement is for organizations to participate in the broader public policy dialogue—tackling corruption, strengthening institutions, and fortifying government frameworks. Often, these are areas where collective action is especially effective; for example, business-led groups have supported efforts from strengthening the criminal justice system in South Africa to promoting the peace and reconciliation processes in Sri Lanka, the Philippines, and Guatemala.

Yet, despite the positive role the global private sector can play in developing countries, operating in insecure areas presents significant challenges: from dealing with corrupt governments to weak infrastructure, potential violence, currency and commodity price swings, shortages of skilled labor, and insufficient legal protections. According to a 2001 survey of the mining industry, when companies were asked why they refrained or withdrew from otherwise sound investments, nearly 80 percent answered that political instability— particularly, armed conflict—was the key reason.[40]

To address such concerns, multilateral institutions, official donors and lenders, NGOs, and private investors must develop new tools to mitigate risk. Though the importance of microfinance programs is well understood, adequate financing remains unavailable for small and medium-sized enterprises—those with between 10 and 100 employees. New mechanisms could be created to help promote the financing of these enterprises by boosting equity or strengthening long-term loans. The aim of such ideas is not to supplant market mechanisms but to create meaningful incentives for private investors to venture into markets they might otherwise write off as hopeless—and, in so doing, help to generate results for poor countries that have embarked on the difficult path of reform.

Just as global corporations are recalibrating their approach to development and social responsibility, so too are NGOs adjusting to new demands. Overall, the pressure for accountability and transparency has affected NGOs as well; the community has responded with self-regulation mechanisms, codes of conduct, more engaged governing boards, public reporting, and other improvements. In addition, NGOs are learning how to operate in a market context—forging partnerships with the private sector on behalf of mutual goals. Oxfam, for example, has helped Unilever analyze its distribution and retail chain in Indonesia, to better appreciate the company's impact, both good and bad, on poverty in that country; and in Venezuela, Amnesty International has joined forces with Statoil and the United Nations Development Program to train judges on human rights issues.

But especially for NGOs working in volatile environments, the past decade has wrought a paradigm shift in their ability to function, as respect for the Red Cross and the Red Crescent and for the Geneva Conventions has eroded and NGO representatives have become the targets of kidnapping, assault, and terror. The cost of providing security for staff members has become a barrier to entry for many humanitarian organizations that otherwise would be on the front lines in insecure areas; for others in uncomfortable proximity to U.S. military stabilization and reconstruction operations, it has forced new thinking and revamped approaches to civil-military relations.

In Iraq—one of the places where humanitarian action and community building are most needed—Mercy Corps is one of only a handful of relief organizations still on the ground. As Nancy Lindborg, president of Mercy Corps, explains, the organization operates entirely on the basis of community acceptance, coinvesting with local communities on the infrastructure and social services they want—whether sewage systems or Internet centers. It takes time and patience for this kind of complex, bottom-up development partnership to take root, but the result is empowered local groups that feel responsible for safeguarding their own achievements.

America's Role: Is Transformational Diplomacy the Route to Security?

For decades, experts have debated whether democracy or development should top the policy agenda. Today, the jury seems to have settled on a commonsense conclusion: Both democracy and development are essential, and neither can endure without the other. And yet, if there is a mounting consensus on the virtues of liberal democracies for economic development and human security, disagreement persists over whether foreign intervention can transplant democracy into societies with weak institutional foundations.

Policymakers clearly need a political strategy to complement their poverty strategy. If poor governance and a lack of accountability are part of the reason that countries are poor in the first place, then simply throwing more money at the problem will not help—and could in fact make the situation worse by reinforcing corruption and the capture of the state by elites. Support for nation building and democracy promotion has been sorely tested in recent years by the United States's struggles in Afghanistan and Iraq, but support for transparent and accountable governance should remain an overarching goal of U.S. foreign assistance. Meanwhile, NGOs and others working at the grass roots can help cultivate poor citizens' familiarity with democratic practices and capacity to hold local officials accountable—even in repressive states, where government-to-government channels are not possible.

Starting in his second term, President George W. Bush has made "transformational diplomacy" the hallmark of his administration's foreign policy—a commitment, in Secretary of State Condoleezza Rice's words, to "work with our many partners around the world to build and sustain democratic, well-governed states that will respond to the needs of their people—and conduct themselves responsibly in the international system."[41] One of the features of transformational diplomacy, also known as the "freedom agenda," is the reorientation of U.S. foreign assistance policy, planning, and oversight toward the goal of democratization.

Although poverty alleviation is not explicitly stated as an objective, Bush administration officials argue that their policy addresses the root cause of hardship. "Achieving transformational development requires more than short-term charity or even the long-term provision of services," Randall Tobias, the administration's new director of foreign assistance, explained in a June 2006 speech. "We must support citizens to make demands of their governments, and reject excuses for failure."[42]

To implement this strategy, the U.S. government is in the midst of reforming and restructuring the way it plans and implements foreign assistance. The process continues reforms and programs launched in the Bush administration's first term—for example, the Office of the Global AIDS Coordinator and the Millennium Challenge Corporation, which together will administer a substantial increase in U.S. foreign aid dollars. The U.S. government is also reforming to improve its response to the varied development and security challenges in states coming out of conflict, in particular through the newly created State Department coordinator for reconstruction and stabilization and new presidential and Department of Defense directives to organize and conduct stability operations in war-torn countries.[43]

It is too soon to judge whether "transformational diplomacy" is a success. The process is still very much under way, and it will need time to find its footing. That said, some challenges to the mission are evident already—from shortfalls that may be alleviated over time, such as the lack of a sufficient talent base among diplomats who are newly supposed to be agents of change; to institutional barriers still to be overcome, such as the traditional divide between "cops" and "caregivers"; to the difficulty of translating the theoretical desirability of democracy into concrete operational plans and programs; to the reality that democratization may produce results that are at loggerheads with U.S. interests—as occurred with Hamas's strong showing in the January 2006 Palestinian elections.

In addition, many observers worry that focusing aid on democratic reforms will neglect the states that are suffering most from poverty and conflict. Democracy is important, but building the institutions required to sustain it takes time; meanwhile, many poor states in conflict confront immediate challenges from pandemic disease to resource scarcities. As Jennifer Windsor of Freedom House explains, "Why are we revisiting whether poor people have to choose between political freedom and freedom from insecurity or freedom from want? If there is anything we have learned over the last twenty years, it is that we need to pursue integrated approaches. The question is how to do that most effectively." The United States will not be applauded for championing democracy if it is perceived as ignoring the deprivation of millions of impoverished people.

There is also a risk that U.S. democracy promotion will be seen as a self-serving strategy designed to bolster America's national security, rather than to lift the lives of needy people around the globe. Critics do not deny the national security benefits of promoting democracy, but they argue for a shift of tone in the way the strategy is advanced—one that assumes more humility and appears less squarely "made-in-the-U.S.A."

Similarly, some humanitarian organizations engaged in development work feel they are on a collision course with the U.S. Agency for International Development (USAID) regarding the "branding" of U.S. foreign assistance. USAID's branding campaign was launched in late 2004, with the aim of helping American taxpayers get "the credit they deserve" for the foreign assistance programs they fund. Presumably, the hope is that global publics will regard the United States more favorably if they understand just how much assistance comes "from the American people," as the revamped USAID tagline reads. To promote the campaign, new federal regulations require all contractors and U.S. NGOs receiving USAID funding to ensure their "programs, projects, activities, public communications, and commodities" prominently bear the USAID standard graphic.

Some experienced NGOs argue, however, that the most effective way to promote sustainable development is to foster the local ownership of programs, and that if America's strategic goal is promoting security and reducing poverty, then the focus should be on empowering effective local change agents, not on getting credit for U.S. taxpayers. As these NGOs suggest, the branding campaign risks undermining the effectiveness of development and democracy programs, because local communities need to feel like they are building something themselves, not be reminded at every turn that their destiny depends on the grace of the United States.

Underlying all these concerns is the continued mismatch between the United States's stated strategic priorities and the way aid dollars are actually spent. A recent analysis by the Brookings Institution in cooperation with the Center for Strategic and International Studies counted more than fifty separate offices addressing more than fifty separate aid objectives (as illustrated in box 1-5)—a laundry list that is not ranked in any consistent hierarchy.

Moreover, the bulk of U.S. assistance does not fund the things the government claims to care about. The United States would like its aid to be progovernance, but even the Middle East Partnership Initiative—the flagship democracy promotion program in that region—represented only 2 percent of overall U.S. economic assistance to the Middle East in 2005; meanwhile, strategically important Egypt received an assistance package amounting to $27 per capita, its autocratic governance notwithstanding. Ghana, in contrast, received less than $4 per capita, even while maintaining relatively good governance.[44]

In 2006, Congress launched the U.S. Commission on Helping to Enhance the Livelihood of People (HELP Commission), whose mandate is to review, over a two-year period, all U.S. foreign assistance and development programs and make recommendations to the U.S. public, president, and Congress on which foreign aid programs work and why, and how U.S. aid dollars can be made most effective. A key challenge for the HELP Commission will be assessing whether development assistance is being allocated to meet its recipients' priorities and needs or to further America's diplomatic and strategic ends. Ideally, the two objectives should complement each other, but the case is not always so clear.

The HELP Commission is determined to avoid the fate of previous evaluations, whose reports, in its words, "end up occupying space on a bookshelf and making little difference in policy."[45] Yet it also acknowledges the difficulty of assessing whether a program's success or failure was the result of its design or implementation. During the past fifty years, the United States has learned some important lessons, yet it still knows less about the effectiveness

BOX 1-5
U.S. Foreign Assistance Objectives and Organizations

Foreign Assistance Objectives

Poverty Reduction
Economic Growth
Business Development
Market Reform
Encourage Foreign Investment
Financial Technical Assistance
International Trade
Job Creation
Democratization
Governance / Rule of Law
Media Freedom
Transparency and Accountability
Monitoring and Evaluation
Child Survival
Strengthen Civil Society
Education
Human Rights
Empowerment of Women
Religious Freedom
Labor Reform
Affordable Nuclear Energy
Nonproliferation
Agricultural Development
Global Health
HIV/AIDS
Tuberculosis and Malaria
Humanitarian Assistance
Disaster Relief
Famine Relief
Migration Assistance
Refugee Assistance
Prevention of Human Trafficking
Antiterrorism
Counternarcotics
Biodiversity Preservation
Natural Resource Management
Ensure Water Access
Sustainable Forest Management
Human Resources Development
Conflict Prevention
Conflict Resolution
Peacekeeping Operations
Stabilization
De-mining Operations
Security
Reconstruction
Infrastructure Construction
Foreign Military Assistance
Scientific and Technological Innovation
Information Technology

U.S. Foreign Assistance Organizations

USAID
Bureau of Democracy, Conflict and Humanitarian Assistance
Office of Democracy and Governance
Office of U.S. Foreign Disaster Assistance and Famine Assistance
Food for Peace
Bureau of Economic Growth, Agriculture and Trade
Bureau of Global Health
Economic Support Fund
Nonproliferation, antiterrorism, de-mining and related programs
International Military Education and Training Program
Office of Transition Initiatives
Famine Early Warning System Network

The Millennium Challenge Corporation

Department of State
Bureau of Democracy, Human Rights and Labor
Office of the Global AIDS Coordinator
Middle East Peace Initiative
Office to Monitor and Combat Trafficking in Persons
Bureau for Population, Refugees and Migration
Office of Political-Military Affairs
Bureau of International Narcotics and Law Enforcement Affairs
Humanitarian Information Unit
Special Coordinator's Office
Bureau of Economic and Business Affairs, Trade Policy and Programs Division
Bureau of Oceans and International Environmental and Scientific Affairs
Office of International Health Affairs

Department of Defense

Department of Treasury
Office of Foreign Asset Controls
Office of Technical Assistance
Office of International Affairs

Department of Health and Human Services
National Institutes of Health
Office of Global Health
Office of International Affairs

Department of Agriculture
Foreign Agricultural Service (Food for Progress, McGovern-Dole Food for Education)
Forest Service

Department of Energy

Department of Commerce

United States Trade Representative

Environmental Protection Agency

Overseas Private Investment Corporation (OPIC)

Peace Corps

U.S. Trade and Development Agency

Export-Import Bank of the United States

FEMA (Office of International Affairs)

U.S. Small Business Administration

African Development Foundation

Inter-American Development Foundation

Office of National Drug Control Policy

of development assistance, or how to measure that effectiveness, than it should. The time is now to invest in development aid impact assessments, so that tomorrow's policymakers have a solid foundation of data on which to base future initiatives.

A Benevolent Web

The challenges of poverty and insecurity are not new. But we now recognize more clearly how much they matter. We have come a long way in understanding the complex relationship between poverty and insecurity, and we have made important strides in solving the problems that stem from them. Yet we still have far to go in addressing the root causes.

Although there is no single pathway out of poverty or toward peace, we can make progress only if we have two basic necessities: good ideas and a common commitment to action. In the words of Brookings president Strobe Talbott, "To address the problem of the tangled web of poverty and insecurity, we need to create a *benevolent* web of NGOs, private sector representatives, governments, and activists."

In fighting against poverty and insecurity, we must confront a range of interconnected issues—from demographics to governance to resource distribution—and embrace a variety of solutions that span the governmental, NGO, and private sectors. Our fight must also include efforts too often relegated to the security field—such as enhancing the capacity for conflict resolution and peacekeeping. There are many new avenues for research that will advance how we understand the difficult problems presented by the complex relationship between poverty and insecurity—and more important, many new opportunities for innovative action to meet these challenges.

But no single person, organization, or country can meet these challenges alone. Only by working together on multiple fronts can we hope to prevail against the scourges of hunger, homelessness, disease, and suffering. Tackling poverty and insecurity is not just a matter of doing the right thing—it is a matter of doing the sensible thing to ensure global security. For the sake of our shared security, for the sake of our shared humanity, there is not a moment to waste.

Notes

1. "The Global Menace of Local Strife," *Economist,* May 24, 2003, 23–25; the citation here is on p. 25.

2. See chapter 2, by Susan E. Rice, in the present volume.

3. Ibid.

4. Stockholm International Peace Research Institute, *SIPRI Yearbook 2006: Armaments, Disarmaments, and International Security* (Oxford University Press, 2006).

5. See chapter 4, by Colin Kahl, in the present volume.

6. Colin Powell, "No Country Left Behind," *Foreign Policy,* January/February 2005, 28–35; the quotation here is on p. 29.

7. National Security Council, "The National Security Strategy of the United States of America," March 2006, 33 (www.whitehouse.gov/nsc/nss/2006/nss2006.pdf [September 2006]).

8. Department of Defense, "Quadrennial Defense Review Report," February 6, 2006, 12 (www.comw.org/qdr/qdr2006.pdf [September 2006]).

9. International Civil Aviation Organization, "Strong Air Traffic Growth Projected Through to 2008," News Release PIO 08/06, Montreal, June 29, 2006.

10. Paul Collier, "The Market for Civil War," *Foreign Policy,* May/June 2003, 38.

11. Edward Miguel, Shanker Satyanath, and Ernest Sergenti, "Economic Shocks and Civil Conflict: An Instrumental Variables Approach," *Journal of Political Economy* 112, no. 4 (2004): 725–53.

12. Susan Rice, "The Threat of Global Poverty," *National Interest,* Spring 2006, 76.

13. "The Global Menace of Local Strife," *Economist,* May 24, 2003, 23.

14. Jason J. Morrissette and Douglas A. Borer, "Where Oil and Water Do Mix: Environmental Scarcity and Future Conflict in the Middle East and North Africa," *Parameters,* Winter 2004–5, 86–101; the citation here is on p. 86.

15. Thomas Homer-Dixon, "Scarcity and Conflict," *Forum for Applied Research and Public Policy* 15, no. 1 (Spring 2000): 28–35; the citation here is on p. 28.

16. Publish What You Pay, "Background," 2004 (www.publishwhatyoupay.org/english/background.shtml [September 2006]).

17. See chapter 4 in the present volume.

18. Simon Robinson, "Nigeria's Deadly Days," *Time International,* May 22, 2006, 20–22.

19. See chapter 3, by Edward Miguel, in the present volume.

20. Publish What You Pay, "Background."

21. See chapter 9, by Jane Nelson, in the present volume.

22. See chapter 7, by Marc Sommers, in the present volume.

23. This number is from chapter 9 in the present volume.

24. This number is found in "Youth and the State of the World," in Global Roundtable Working Group on Youth (www.advocatesforyouth.org/PUBLICATIONS/factsheet/fsstateworld.pdf [September 2006]).

25. This number is from chapter 9 in the present volume.

26. This number is found in "Stress Factor One: The Youth Bulge," by Richard Cincotta, Robert Engelman, and Daniele Anastasion, in *The Security Demographic: Population and Civil Conflict after the Cold War* (Washington: Population Action International, 2003), 43.

27. See chapter 6, by Henrik Urdal, in the present volume.

28. Paul Collier, "Doing Well Out of War: An Economic Perspective," in *Greed & Grievance: Economic Agendas in Civil Wars,* ed. Mats Berdal and David M. Malone (Boulder, Colo.: Lynne Rienner, 2000), 91–111.

29. Jack A. Goldstone, "Demography, Environment, and Security," in *Environmental Conflict,* ed. Paul F. Diehl and Nils Petter Gleditsch (Boulder, Colo.: Westview Press, 2001), 84–108.

30. See chapter 6 in the present volume.

31. See chapter 7 in the present volume.

32. Youth Business International, "YBI Information Sheet: Youth Employment through Entrepreneurship" (www.youth-business.org/MainFrame.aspx?MenuID=1& pagename=contentpage.aspx&LinkID=53 [September 2006]).

33. Robert I. Rotberg, "Strengthening African Leadership," *Foreign Affairs,* July/August 2004, 14–18; the citation here is on p. 14.

34. Joshua Hammer, "Big Man: Is the Mugabe Era Near Its End?" *New Yorker,* June 26, 2006, 28–34; the citation here is on p. 29.

35. See chapter 8, by Robert I. Rotberg, in the present volume.

36. United Nations Development Program, "Mauritius: Country Sheet," *Human Development Report* data, 2006 (http://hdr.undp.org/statistics/data/countries.cmf?c=MUS [September 2006]).

37. Republic of Mozambique, "Report on the Millennium Development Goals," August 2005.

38. Ken Hackett, Address to the Baltimore Council on Foreign Affairs, Baltimore, June 7, 2006. Reprinted in *Vital Speeches of the Day,* August 2006.

39. "Role of Business in Armed Conflict Can Be Crucial, 'for Good and for Ill,' Secretary-General Tells Security Council Open Debate on Issue," United Nations Press Release SG/SM/9256-SC/8059, April 15, 2005.

40. Jason Switzer, "Conflicting Interests," *Elements,* August 2001, 10–12; the citation here is on p. 10.

41. Condoleezza Rice, "Transformational Diplomacy," lecture at Georgetown University School of Foreign Service, January 18, 2006.

42. Randall Tobias, "Getting a Better Return on America's Investment in People," remarks at the Initiative for Global Development 2006 National Summit, June 15, 2006.

43. For example, see "National Security Presidential Directive/NSPD-44," December 7, 2005 (www.fas.org/irp/offdocs/nspd/nspd-44.pdf [September 2006]); and "Department of Defense Directive 3000.05," November 28, 2005 (www.dtic.mil/whs/directives/corres/pdf/d300005_112805/d300005p.pdf [September 2006]).

44. Lael Brainard, "A Unified Framework for U.S. Foreign Assistance," in *Security by Other Means* (Brookings, 2007), 8–16.

45. U.S. Commission on Helping to Enhance the Livelihood of People, "When and How Will the Commission Do Its Work?" (http://helpcommission.gov/MyiBelong/EditAbout/When/tabid/66/Default.aspx [September 2006]).

2

Poverty Breeds Insecurity

S∪SAN E. RICE

FEW AMERICAN LEADERS today evince much interest in poverty—either domestic or international. Contrast our current obsession with flag burning, the estate tax, immigration, or gay marriage with the animating themes of the 1960s. Then, John and Robert Kennedy, Lyndon Johnson, Martin Luther King Jr., and many others summoned our national energy to wage a "War on Poverty" and build a "Great Society." Our media brought us searing images of destitution from Appalachia to the Mississippi Delta to the South Bronx. Our president insisted in global forums that "political sovereignty is but a mockery without the means of meeting poverty and illiteracy and disease. Self-determination is but a slogan if the future holds no hope."[1]

With domestic poverty less visible but no less real and global poverty dismissed by many as the inevitable fate of the black, brown, and yellow wretched of the earth, the majority of Americans seem, variously, tired or ignorant of, or indifferent to, a scourge that kills millions across our planet every year. Yet, in Britain, Labour and Conservative party leaders compete on the basis of their commitment to fight global poverty. Public awareness of this issue in Britain would confound most Americans. Perhaps Britons have been so relentlessly bombarded by Bono, Bob Geldof, the BBC, Gordon Brown, and Tony Blair that many have come to recognize the linkages between their own security and prosperity and that of peoples in remote corners of the planet. Americans do not yet, and it is past time that they should.

Poverty and Insecurity

Grinding poverty is the lot of half the world's population. Three billion human beings subsist on less than $2 per day—$730 a year—the equivalent of seven pairs of quality sneakers in the United States. In the developing world, poverty is not just a sentence to misery; it can often be a sentence to death. Hunger, malnutrition, and easily preventable diseases like diarrhea, respiratory infections, malaria, and cholera thrive in fetid slums that have no basic sewerage, clean water, or electricity, while desolate rural areas lack basic health infrastructure to provide prenatal care or lifesaving vaccines. According to UNICEF, 10.5 million children *under five years old* die *each year* from preventable illnesses—30,000 *each day*—ten times the number who perished in the attacks of September 11, 2001. The vast majority of these children succumb, in effect, to poverty. Children living in the poorest 20 percent of households are two to three times more likely to die than those living in the richest 20 percent in the same countries.[2]

Basic intuition suggests that such pervasive poverty and grotesque disparities breed resentment, hostility, and insecurity. Nevertheless, a significant amount of punditry and even academic effort has been devoted to discrediting the notion that poverty has any security consequence for Americans.[3] The most frequently invoked canards draw on oversimplified truisms, such as poverty does not cause terrorism, because the 9/11 hijackers were mainly middle-class, educated Saudis; if poor people were prone to be terrorists, then Africa and not the Middle East would be the hotbed of terrorism; and poor people are too busy just trying to survive to do anyone harm. All these statements are superficial and flawed, but assume for a moment they are true. Assume that an individual's economic impoverishment has nothing to do with his or her decisions about whether or not to engage in acts of violence. Would that be a rational basis for concluding that global poverty has no security significance to the United States? Some would have us believe so, but they would be mistaken.

For even if poverty *at the individual level* were of no security significance to the United States and other developed countries (dubious though that proposition is), poverty is highly significant *at the country level*.[4] Poor states typically fail to meet the basic needs of many of their citizens—for food, clean water, health care, or education. Where human needs are great and service gaps persist, people tend to accept help from almost anyone willing to provide it. Sometimes, help comes from multilateral or bilateral aid agencies.

Sometimes, it comes from secular nongovernmental organizations (NGOs). But in Africa and South Asia, food, clothing, schools, and health care are often provided by foreign-funded religious NGOs, Christian missionaries or mosques—sometimes with theological, even extremist, strings attached. These same poor states that cannot fulfill their core responsibilities to provide security or sustenance to their own people may also fail to exercise effective sovereign control over their territory. Poor states often lack the legal, police, intelligence, or security sector capacity to control their borders and remote areas and to prevent plundering of their natural resources.

Poor states can be high-risk zones that in a rapidly globalizing world may eventually, often indirectly, pose significant risks to faraway countries. How? People, goods, funds, and information now traverse the planet with lightning speed. More than 2 million travelers cross an international border each day. Between 1994 and 2006, air traffic volume is estimated to have nearly doubled from 2.1 trillion passenger-kilometers flown to 3.95 trillion passenger-kilometers.[5] Since 1970, total seaborne trade is estimated to have almost tripled.[6] These factors combine to increase Americans' exposure to distant phenomena—transnational security threats that can arise from and spread to anywhere on the planet.

These threats could take various forms: a mutated avian flu virus that jumps from poultry to humans in Cambodia or Burkina Faso; a U.S. expatriate who unwittingly contracts Marburg virus in Angola and returns to Houston on an oil company charter flight; a terrorist cell that attacks a U.S. Navy vessel in Yemen or Somalia; the theft of biological or nuclear materials from poorly secured facilities in the former Soviet Union; narcotics traffickers in Tajikistan and criminal syndicates from Nigeria; or, over the longer term, flooding and other effects of global warming exacerbated by extensive deforestation in the Amazon and Congo River basins. Weak states such as these can function *passively* as potential incubators or conveyor belts for transnational threats. Dangerous spillovers from weak states could result in major damage to the U.S. economy. In a worst-case scenario, such as a deadly pandemic, they could result in the loss of hundreds of thousands—if not millions—of American lives.

Which States Are Weak, and Why?

The world's weakest states are typically poor states that lack the capacity to fulfill essential government functions, chiefly (1) to secure their population from violent conflict, (2) to competently meet the basic human needs of their population (that is, food, health, education), (3) to govern legitimately and effectively with the acceptance of a majority of their population, and (4) to foster sustainable and equitable economic growth. Descriptions of the universe of weak states vary. The British Department for International Development, the Fund for Peace, the World Bank, and others have defined substantially overlapping but differing sets of "weak," "fragile," "failing," or "low-income . . . under stress" states. In some instances, the countries are not listed publicly or the rationale for their inclusion is left unstated to avoid political controversy.

In 2006, Susan Rice and Stewart Patrick initiated a collaborative project called the "Weak States Threat Matrix." We have begun identifying the world's weakest states based on clear-cut and transparent criteria. We will subsequently assess the nature and significance of the transnational security threats that can or do emanate from each of these countries. Our purpose is to provide policymakers with an analytical basis for differentiating among the large number of weak states and for prioritizing the allocation of scarce attention and resources.

The drivers of state weakness vary enormously from state to state. Poverty fundamentally erodes state capacity—by fueling conflict, sapping human capital, by hollowing out or impeding the development of effective state institutions and markets, and by creating especially conducive environments for corrupt governance. Though poverty underlies state weakness, weakness is also a consequence of other capacity deficits: a lack of political legitimacy, a lack of competence in economic governance and in the adequate provision of essential services to the population, and a lack of security as evidenced by conflict and instability. Each of these capacity gaps can, in turn, exacerbate poverty (figure 2-1).

Susan Rice and Stewart Patrick's research collaboration identifies the weakest states as those that suffer from the most significant deficits in security, economic performance, social welfare, and political legitimacy.

A preliminary analysis shows that the preponderance of the world's weakest states is found in Africa, Central Asia, and South Asia (figure 2-2). They include Afghanistan, Algeria, Angola, Bangladesh, Burkina Faso, Burundi, Cambodia, Cameroon, Central African Republic, Chad, Colombia, Comoros, Democratic Republic of the Congo, Côte d'Ivoire, Djibouti, East Timor, Equitorial Guinea, Eritrea, Ethiopia, Gambia, Guatemala, Guinea, Guinea-Bissau, Haiti, India, Indonesia, Iraq, Kenya, Laos, Liberia, Madagascar,

Figure 2-1. State of Capacity Deficits

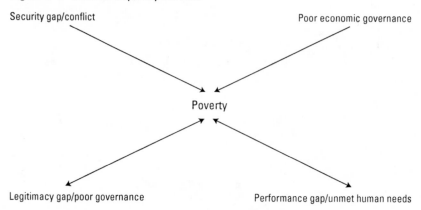

Malawi, Mali, Mauritania, Mozambique, Myanmar, Nepal, Niger, Nigeria, North Korea, Pakistan, Papua New Guinea, Philippines, Republic of Congo, Rwanda, Sierra Leone, Solomon Islands, Somalia, Sri Lanka, Sudan, Swaziland, Tajikistan, Tanzania, Togo, Turkmenistan, Uganda, Uzbekistan, Yemen, Zambia, and Zimbabwe.

There is a second tier of states that also warrant close scrutiny, because they may still serve as significant breeding grounds for transnational security threats. Among these are Cuba, Egypt, and Iran.

Weak states can be classified into four categories: autocracies; conflict countries; countries transitioning from conflict or autocracy; and fragile, young democracies that appear to be on a path to sustainable security, if not yet broad-based development. These classifications are admittedly fluid, and some states may not fall squarely into any single category but rather straddle the gray areas between or among them. Nonetheless, the objective of U.S. and international policy should be to help weak states move from conflict and autocracy, through postconflict or postautocratic transitional periods, to the more stable stage of fragile, functioning democracy (figure 2-3).

The ultimate policy goal should be to build the ranks of capable states—such as Botswana, Chile, Mauritius, Romania, Poland, and Thailand—that attain at least middle-income status, consolidate democracy, and achieve lasting peace (for at least a generation), while contributing constructively to the international system.

Figure 2-2. Map of Weak States

Source: Based on author's rankings of weak states.

Figure 2-3. Weak States Differ Significantly

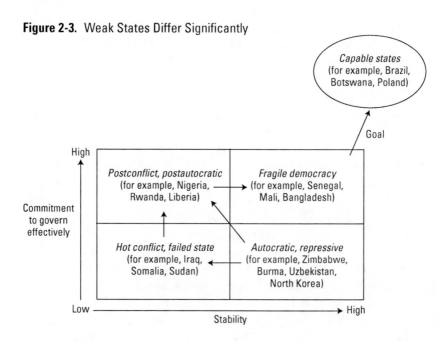

Transnational "Spillovers" from Weak States

Weak states hobbled by poverty and, often, by poor governance, pose the most immediate and deadly risks to their own citizens. These dangers can include violence, corruption, and governmental neglect or abuse. Yet, in a globalizing world that must contend increasingly with transnational security threats even more often than state-based threats, the consequences of state weakness can and do spill over borders into neighboring countries and even to far-flung regions of the world.

Conflict

Among the most significant consequences of country-level poverty is heightened risk of conflict. Poor countries are much more likely than rich countries to experience civil war. Recent statistical research on poverty and conflict suggests that for a country at the 50th percentile for income (like Iran today), the risk of experiencing civil conflict within five years is 7–11 percent; for countries at the 10th percentile (like Ghana or Uganda today), the risk rises to 15–18 percent.[7] A wide range of empirical research finds that per capita

GDP has an important, statistically significant relationship with the likelihood of civil war outbreak.[8] The link between poverty and conflict is a rare area of emerging scholarly consensus and probably the most robust finding in the econometric literature on conflict.[9]

Put simply, increasing a country's GDP—without changing other important factors such as the degree of democratization or number of ethnic groups—reduces the chance of civil war in that country. An otherwise "average" country with $250 GDP per capita has a 15 percent risk of experiencing a civil war in the next five years, whereas for a country with per capita GDP of $5,000, the risk of civil war drops to less than 1 percent over the same period.[10] Other potential poverty-related conflict risk factors include shrinking economic growth, low levels of education, and high child mortality rates.

The case of Sierra Leone is illustrative. Just before civil war broke out there in March 1991, economic growth was negative and real GDP per capita had dropped more than 35 percent from 1970s levels.[11] Sierra Leone in 1990 ranked last on the UN Human Development Index. Youth unemployment had soared and the education system, once among the best in the region, had collapsed with the economic decline of the 1980s. Lacking opportunities to pursue responsible employment, disaffected youth were more easily drawn to rebel activity as a means of gaining power and income looted from civilians and the country's rich alluvial diamond fields.[12]

When conflict breaks out, poverty can help perpetuate the fighting, and once a conflict has ended, poverty may also increase the likelihood that it will recur.[13] The resumption of violence in East Timor in 2006, which displaced an estimated 150,000, underscores this risk. Many experts lauded East Timor as reliably on the path to lasting peace, but they failed to weigh the security consequences of its persistent poverty. Seven years into the postconflict period, poverty jumped following the departure of the large UN presence four years ago, which had artificially boosted economic activity. Despite substantial international aid inflows, relatively little was devoted to improving basic health services or stimulating job-creating investment. East Timor's child mortality rate remains among the highest in the world, and more than 50 percent of young men and many veterans have no jobs, heating a cauldron of disaffected youth.[14]

Civil wars tend to be long, and their resolution often falters. By one estimate, civil wars last an average of sixteen years.[15] One-third of those that end later reignite.[16] Thus, poor countries can fall into a vicious cycle termed the "conflict trap."[17] This trap can be broken or avoided when economic performance improves in postconflict countries. Mozambique exemplifies the alternative path. In the years since the war ended in 1994, Mozambique, one of the world's poorest nations, has achieved average annual GDP growth of 8.1 percent, according to the World Bank. Gross primary school enrollment jumped from 60 percent in 1995 to roughly full enrollment for the period 2003–5. Sustained economic growth and investments in social services contributed to a 16 percent reduction in poverty from 1997 to 2003.[18] More than a decade after the cessation of conflict, Mozambique appears to be among the more stable young democracies in Southern Africa.

When conflicts ignite, they function as the ultimate killer of innocents. They also can be sinkholes that destabilize entire regions, as did Liberia and Congo, and require costly international peacekeeping and humanitarian interventions. At the same time, conflict zones provide the optimal anarchic environment for transnational predators: international criminals, as in Haiti and Moldova; drug producers and smugglers, as in Afghanistan, Colombia, and Tajikistan; weapons traffickers, as in Somalia and West Africa; international terrorists, as in Bosnia, Iraq, and Sudan; and deadly pathogens, as in Angola, Congo, and Uganda.

Terrorism

Most dangerous are those conflict zones that collapse into fully failed states, which lose the ability to control much of their territory. Afghanistan and, most recently, Somalia are classic failed states where anarchy facilitated the ascendancy of Islamic extremists who gained their foothold by defeating warlords and providing essential social services to bereft populations. Before the June 2006 takeover by the radical wing of the Islamic Courts Union, Somalia served as an operational base for al Qaeda–linked terrorists. The perpetrators of "Black Hawk Down" are believed to have received arms and training from al Qaeda for the 1993 attack on U.S. forces. Several al Qaeda operatives implicated in the East Africa embassy bombings have taken refuge in Somalia. Arms smuggled from Somalia were used in the 2002 Mombasa attacks. More recently, terrorists with ties to al Qaeda killed a series of Western civilians in Somaliland, Mogadishu, and other parts of the country.[19]

Yet weak states need not collapse into conflict or fail before they can be exploited by terrorist groups. Al Qaeda has preyed on the territory, cash crops, natural resources, and financial institutions of low-income but comparatively more stable states from Senegal to Yemen. Militants exploited poor immigration, security, and financial controls to plan and carry out terrorist operations in Kenya, Tanzania, and Indonesia. It is estimated that al Qaeda and its affiliates operate in approximately sixty countries worldwide.[20]

Mali is an example of a well-governed country that suffers from capacity gaps that extremist groups have been able to exploit. Ninety percent Muslim and a multiparty democracy since 1992, Mali cooperates fully with the United States on counterterrorism matters. It remains, however, an extremely poor state with gross national income per capita of $380.[21] An estimated 72 percent of its almost 12 million people live on less than $1 per day, and income inequality is high. Mali's human development ranked the fourth lowest in the world in 2005.[22] Landlocked and bordering seven states—Mauritania, Algeria, Côte d'Ivoire, Guinea, Senegal, Burkina Faso, and Niger—Mali is roughly the size of Texas plus California. Malian authorities have struggled, often without success, to prevent al-Qaeda-linked terrorists of the Algerian-based Salafist Group for Preaching and Combat (GSPC) from operating on their territory. Mali's poorly controlled borders, nomadic populations, vast uninhabited spaces, and underresourced security services render it an attractive recruiting, training, and hiding place for the GSPC. Its leader, Amari Saifi (known as "El Para") and his associates evaded capture in the Northern Malian desert for six months before releasing thirty-two European hostages seized in southern Algeria. The GSPC also utilizes Mali's centuries-old trans-Saharan Tuareg trading routes to smuggle cigarettes and other contraband to raise cash for operations.[23]

Mali's poverty renders it vulnerable to terrorist infiltration in another critical way. Like several poor, weak states with large Muslim populations (for example, Pakistan, Bangladesh, Somalia, and Nigeria), Mali's government lacks the resources and institutional capacity to provide adequately for its citizens. Large numbers do not have enough to eat or have access to potable water, basic medical care, or educational opportunities for their children. In Mali, as elsewhere, the social services gap is being filled by outsiders, often Wahhabist charities and mosques funded from the Gulf States. As Abass Haidara, imam of the historic Sankore Mosque in Timbuktu, explained: Wahhabists are setting up mosques all over northern Mali, often right next door to the indigenous Sufi mosques. They offer what the Sufis cannot— food, clothing, medical care, schools, and the opportunity to send young men to Saudi Arabia for religious training. When those newly minted Wahhabist clerics return, they draw additional adherents to their extremist ideology. The Wahhabists, Haidara says, take the long view—over generations—as they slowly work to drive the traditional mosques out of existence.[24]

There is recent evidence that al Qaeda strategists deliberately target weak, poor states. The Combating Terrorism Center of the U.S. Military Academy at West Point calls *The Management of Savagery: The Most Critical Stage through Which the Umma Will Pass* "one of the most recent and significant" jihadi strategic texts. In it, Abu Bakr Naji outlines successive stages in establishing an Islamic caliphate. A key stage, "the management of savagery," aims to bring order, security, and Islamic sharia rule to formerly chaotic states, such as pre-Taliban Afghanistan, so they can form the foundation of an eventual caliphate. Naji writes: "The states initially designated for inclusion in the group of priority regions are the regions of the following states: Jordan, the countries of the Maghrib, Nigeria, Pakistan, and the countries of the Haramayn and the Yemen." The "common links between states in which the regions of savagery can come into being" include "the weakness of the ruling regime and the weakness of the centralization of its power in the peripheries of the borders of its state and sometimes in internal regions, particularly those that are over-crowded" and "the presence of jihadi, Islamic expansion being propagated in these regions."[25]

Similarly, a 2006 article by Abu Azzam al-Ansari, titled "Al Qaeda Moving to Africa," in *Sada al-Jihad,* an online jihadi magazine, cites the weakness of Africa's states and pervasive corruption as an advantage, making it an easier place to operate than "in other countries which have effective security, intelligence and military capacities." The same author also writes that Africa's poverty and social conditions "will enable the mujahadeen to provide some finance and welfare, thus, posting there some of their influential operatives."[26]

Disease

Poverty increases the risk of human exposure to pathogens and severely constrains poor countries' capacity to prevent, detect, and treat deadly disease outbreaks or to contain them before they spread abroad. The incidence of deaths due to infectious disease is rising. Twice the number of Americans (170,000) died of infectious diseases in 2000 as in 1980.[27] Of the roughly thirty new infectious diseases that have emerged globally over the past three decades, many—such as SARS, West Nile virus, HIV/AIDS, hepatitis C, and H5N1 avian flu virus—originated in developing countries that had rudimentary disease surveillance capability.

Growing population pressure impels people seeking arable land, firewood, and water to press more deeply into previously uninhabited areas. The risk of human exposure to zoonotic diseases consequently increases. Poor families in developing countries also often live in close proximity to their livestock, which provide sustenance and income. Chickens and pigs have proved the source of deadly diseases that jump from animal to human. H5N1 avian flu is the most alarming recent example. Should that virus mutate into a form easily transmissible from human to human, the threat of a global pandemic becomes imminent. With mortality rates currently exceeding 50 percent, if a mutated virus retains the virulence of current strains, it could kill tens of millions worldwide. As of July 4, 2006, the H5N1 virus had been confirmed in humans or animals in at least forty-eight countries, including some of the most impoverished, remote, and poorly governed parts of Asia and Africa (for example, Burkina Faso, Cambodia, Côte d'Ivoire, Indonesia, Laos, Myanmar, Nigeria, Niger, Sudan, and Vietnam), adding to fears that the virus could mutate as a result of contact between animals and humans.[28] At the same time, if a deadly mutation first occurs in a country with a weak health care infrastructure, the odds of detecting and swiftly containing the outbreak are reduced.

The Democratic Republic of the Congo (DRC) is one of several Central African epicenters of disease. Congo experienced its first known outbreak of deadly hemorrhagic Ebola fever, which the World Health Organization characterizes as "one of the most virulent diseases known to mankind," in 1976. The fatality rate was roughly 90 percent. More recent outbreaks in 1995, 2002, and 2005 killed at least 75 percent of their victims.[29] The Ebola strain that first emerged in the DRC spread to Gabon, Uganda, and South Africa. It has the potential to travel anywhere in the world because it is highly transmissible by contact with bodily fluids (including blood, sweat, and saliva) and has an incubation period of two to twenty-one days.[30]

Congo is uniquely ill equipped to detect, treat, and contain disease. Its population is extremely vulnerable (with 71 percent malnourished in 2000–2, up from 32 percent a decade earlier and roughly 20 percent under-five mortality).[31] The DRC's per capita expenditure on the health sector is the lowest of any country in the world ($14 per person in terms of purchasing power parity).[32] The continuing conflict in Eastern Congo and the presence of approximately 17,500 UN peacekeepers increases the possibility that foreign military, police, or aid workers could contract infectious agents and transport them abroad. For instance, a June 2006 suspected outbreak of pneumonic plague in the violent Ituri region, where UN forces have been active, sickened 100 and killed almost 20 percent of its victims.[33] If a disease is detected early enough, antibiotics can treat the disease, which is contracted through contact with infected rodents or fleas or by the airborne transmission of bacteria. Unfortunately, the DRC's poor surveillance and control mechanisms make early treatment less likely, particularly because conflict impedes access for international health workers.

Although Ebola and the similar Marburg virus have not yet spread beyond Africa, other new or reemergent infectious diseases have. These include polio, which was almost eradicated before spreading to Indonesia from northern Nigeria in 2004–05. The occasionally deadly West Nile virus, a mosquito-borne disease that originated in Uganda, reached New York City in 1999 presumably by aircraft, and it is now found throughout the continental United States. Rift Valley fever spread from East Africa to Yemen and Saudi Arabia in 2000, infecting hundreds and killing 11 percent of the people it infected in Yemen, and 19 percent of infected people in Saudi Arabia.[34] Lassa hemorrhagic fever, endemic to West Africa, particularly the Mano River region, infects an estimated 100,000 to 300,000 people each year with flu-like symptoms.[35] Fatality rates can reach 15 to 20 percent, especially among hospitalized patients, where human-to-human transmission can occur via blood or human secretions. There have been several fatal cases among UN peacekeepers deployed to bring stability to Liberia and Sierra Leone.[36] An estimated 20 cases of Lassa have been reported outside of Africa, including one American businessman who perished upon returning to the United States. Before he died, he came into direct contact with 188 people in the United States while his fever was believed to be contagious. None of them died.[37]

Inadequate health care infrastructure hampers disease detection and containment not only in Africa, but also in the poorest, weakest states around the world. Bangladesh, which remains poor, has made important gains in some aspects of its social infrastructure but still spends relatively little per capita on health (about $68 in terms of purchasing power parity as of 2003)—the same amount as Burkina Faso and less than North Korea.[38] Its lack of capacity in the health sector may have contributed to Bangladesh's difficulty in investigating five outbreaks of the Nipah virus since 2001, which first appeared in Malaysia and has resulted in fatality rates as high as 75 percent. The virus is not known to have spread from Bangladesh, though it is fairly contagious and has a relatively long incubation period.

In Latin America and the Caribbean, mosquito-borne dengue fever, including the deadly hemorrhagic variety, is resurgent, afflicting locals and foreign travelers in growing numbers. Dengue's global distribution and impact on humans is now deemed comparable to malaria by the Centers for Disease Control and Prevention, except in Africa. Dengue is believed to have first appeared in the Western Hemisphere in Brazil via mosquito-infested ships from South East Asia in the 1990s. Urbanization, population growth, and a deteriorating public health infrastructure have increased the prevalence of dengue in Central and South America.[39] The *Aedes* mosquito, which carries the virus, is now common in parts of the U.S. South and Southwest. As the U.S. climate warms, dengue will likely spread further within the United States.

Environmental Degradation

The relationship between poverty, state weakness, and environmental degradation is complex and mutually reinforcing. Population growth is fastest in the developing world. Poverty can prompt families to produce more children to counter high infant mortality rates and to increase income. Population pressure, in turn, heightens the demand for arable land for subsistence and cash crops as well as for energy. Energy consumption in the poorest countries often takes the form of wood burning. The demand for arable land combines with firewood gathering and logging for precious hardwoods to accelerate deforestation. Weak states typically lack the will and the means to prevent peasants, farmers, or even foreign logging operations from chopping down forests and woodlands. Moreover, in war zones, like Liberia and Cambodia, precious hardwoods have been logged and sold in large quantities to fund conflict. The result is the loss of tree cover at alarming rates in many of the poorest states from Nigeria to the Congo River basin to Laos. According to the Food and Agriculture Organization, deforestation is costing the world an estimated 13 million hectares of forest (the rough equivalent of Panama or South Carolina) each year, mostly in South America and Africa.[40]

Haiti and Madagascar dramatize the relationship between poverty and environmental degradation. With a per capita GDP of $361 and an estimated 65 percent of its population living below the national poverty line, Haiti is the poorest country in the Western Hemisphere.[41] One of the few sources of fuel there is firewood, and cutting down trees to make charcoal provides a rare source of income. Peasant farmers exacerbate the problem, as they clear land to try to feed their families. As a result, in stark contrast to the more affluent Dominican Republic next door, Haiti is now 90 percent deforested; 30 million trees are cut down each year.[42] The tree cover in Haiti has plummeted from approximately 60 percent in 1923 to less than 2 percent at present.[43] The 2004 floods that resulted in mudslides that killed an estimated 3,000 Haitians after Tropical Storm Jeanne indicate the deadly short-term consequences of extreme deforestation. Though most of this logging is not legal, the fragile Haitian government does not have the resources to enforce its own laws.

In even poorer Madagascar, the practice of "tavy," or slash-and-burn agriculture, by subsistence farmers and cattle herders has contributed to the loss of 80 percent of the country's tropical rainforest cover. Erosion causes Madagascar's rivers to run red into the Indian Ocean.[44] Logging, often illegal, of valuable Malagasy ebony and rosewood intensifies deforestation. Between 1990 and 2005, Madagascar lost 14.3 percent of its forest and woodland habitat.[45] This rapid loss, now estimated to be 1 percent of remaining forests per year, is especially worrying, because the country is a tremendous source of global biodiversity. The island contains at least 13,000 different species of plant, of which 89 percent are endemic to it. A comparably high rate of its mammals, reptiles, and amphibians is unique to the island, and scientists are still discovering new species there.[46]

The adverse global consequences of deforestation are multiple and serious. Erosion exacerbates flooding and causes the silting of waterways. Soil degradation reduces agricultural yields and thus increases hunger. Precious biodiversity is irreparably lost. Forests, which contain half the world's biodiversity, hold the key to curing many deadly diseases. For example, Madagascar's native, endangered rosy periwinkle plant is used to treat leukemia and Hodgkin's disease.[47] Deforestation leads to drought and disrupts the hydrologic cycle in tropical rainforests by reducing the evaporative cooling facilitated by moist canopy cover.

Finally, deforestation accelerates climate change. Though fossil fuel burning in developed and emerging countries accounts for the majority of global carbon emissions (totaling an estimated 6 billion metric tons a year), according to the U.S. National Aeronautics and Space Administration, deforestation is responsible for more than 25 percent, or 1.6 billion metric tons of carbon released annually into the atmosphere.[48] Forests are "carbon sinks" that store carbon from the atmosphere; their loss reduces global carbon absorption capacity. Cut and rotting trees or stumps, moreover, release additional carbon that joins with oxygen to become carbon dioxide (CO_2). Burning of trees for fuel and other purposes compounds CO_2 emissions. As global temperatures rise because of these atmospheric changes, coastal areas become more vulnerable to flooding, lakes dry up, and some landlocked areas grow more prone to severe drought, which, in turn, increases the risk of instability and intensifies poverty. Indigenous species get driven from their natural habitat, coral reefs become bleached, and disease vectors change, bringing once tropical illnesses into temperate zones.

Conclusion

Environmental degradation is but one of the several serious consequences of persistent global poverty and weak state capacity. The fact that the impact of poverty and weak states on U.S. and global security is not simple, linear, or necessarily swift does not make the linkage any less real or significant. Efforts to illuminate the complex relationship between poverty and insecurity may be unwelcome to those who want assurance that global poverty and U.S. national security are unrelated. Yet we ignore or obscure the implications of global poverty for global security at our peril.

Notes

1. John F. Kennedy, "Address before the General Assembly of the United Nations," September 25, 1961.

2. United Nations Children's Fund, *State of the World's Children 2006: Excluded and Invisible* (New York: United Nations, 2006), 19–20.

3. Among the pundits, see, for instance, Daniel Pipes, "It's Not the Economy, Stupid: What the West Needs to Know about the Rise of Radical Islam," *Washington Post,* July 2, 1995. Among academics, see Alan Krueger and Jitka Maleckova, "Education, Poverty and Terrorism: Is There a Causal Connection?" *Journal of Economic Perspectives* 17, no. 4 (Fall 2002): 119–44; and James Piazza, "Poverty, Political Freedom and the Roots of Terrorism," *American Economic Review (Papers and Proceedings)* 96, no. 2 (May 2006): 50–56.

4. Parts of this chapter have been adapted from Susan E. Rice, "The Threat of Global Poverty," *National Interest,* Spring 2006, 76–82.

5. International Civil Aviation Organization, "World Air Passenger Traffic to Continue to Expand through 2007," ICAO News Release, July 28, 2005. Note that the figures for 2006 are a projection.

6. United Nations Conference on Trade and Development, *Review of Maritime Transport, 2006* (New York: United Nations, 2006).

7. Paul Collier and Anke Hoeffler, two prominent scholars working on the political economy of conflict, estimate the risk to be 7.5 percent at the 50th percentile for GDP per capita, and 15 percent at the 10th percentile; Paul Collier, Anke Hoeffler, and Mans Soderbom, "On the Duration of Civil War," *Journal of Peace Research* 41, no. 3 (2004): 253–73. Two other prominent scholars, James D. Fearon and David D. Laitin, estimate the risk for countries at the 50th percentile in terms of income to be 10.7 percent, and 17.7 percent for countries at the 10th percentile; James D. Fearon and David D. Laitin, "Ethnicity, Insurgency, and Civil War," *American Political Science Review* 97, no. 1 (2003): 75–90. Illustrative examples of countries at the 10th and 50th percentile in terms of GDP per capita in 2005 dollars were drawn from the IMF's World Economic Outlook Database, September 2006 edition (www.imf.org/external/pubs/ft/weo/2006/02/data/index. aspx [December 2006]).

8. For a recent review of this literature and its policy implications, see Susan E. Rice, Corinne Graff, and Janet Lewis, *Poverty and Civil War: What Policymakers Need to Know,* Brookings Global Economy and Development Working Paper 2 (Brookings, 2006).

9. See Macartan Humphreys and Ashutosh Varshney, "Violent Conflict and the Millennium Development Goals: Diagnosis and Recommendations," paper prepared for meeting of Millennium Development Goals Poverty Task Force Workshop, Bangkok, 2004; Nicholas Sambanis, "Poverty and the Organization of Political Violence: A Review and Some Conjectures," in *Brookings Trade Forum 2004: Globalization, Poverty, and*

Inequality, ed. Susan Collins and Carol Graham (Brookings, 2004); and Nicholas Sambanis, "What Is Civil War? Conceptual and Empirical Complexities of an Operational Definition," *Journal of Conflict Resolution* 48, no. 6 (2004): 814–58.

10. These figures were estimated in Macartan Humphreys, "Economics and Violent Conflict" (Department of Economics, Harvard University, 2003), using data found in Paul Collier and Anke Hoeffler, "On the Incidence of Civil War in Africa," *Journal of Conflict Resolution* 46, no. 1 (2002): 13–28. The figures are frequently cited by the U.K.'s Department for International Development and are found in Prime Minister's Strategy Unit, "Investing in Prevention: An International Strategy to Manage Risks of Instability and Improve Crisis Response," *A Prime Minister's Strategy Unit Report to the Government of the U.K.,* February 2005.

11. Nicholas Sambanis, "Using Case Studies to Expand Economic Models of Civil War," *Perspectives on Politics* 2, no. 2 (June 2004): 259–79.

12. UN High Commissioner for Refugees, "Sierra Leone: From Cease-Fire to Lasting Peace?" *WRITENET Report* (www.unhcr.org/publ/RSDCOI/3ae6a6b624.html [December 2006]).

13. On poverty and the duration of conflict, see Collier, Hoeffler, and Soderbom, "On the Duration of Civil War"; and James D. Fearon, "Why Do Some Civil Wars Last So Much Longer than Others?" *Journal of Peace Research* 41, no. 3 (2004): 275–301. On poverty and the recurrence of conflict, see Barbara F. Walter, "Does Conflict Beget Conflict? Explaining Recurring Civil War," *Journal of Peace Research* 41, no. 3 (2004): 371–88.

14. Arnold Kohen and Lawrence Korb, "The World Must Heed the Harsh Lessons of East Timor," *Financial Times,* June 30, 2006.

15. Fearon, "Why Do Some Civil Wars Last So Much Longer than Others?"

16. Walter, "Does Conflict Beget Conflict?"

17. World Bank, *Breaking the Conflict Trap: Civil War and Development Policy,* World Bank Policy Research Report (Oxford University Press, 2003).

18. World Bank, *World Bank Country Brief: Mozambique* (http://web.worldbank.org/ WBSITE/EXTERNAL/COUNTRIES/AFRICAEXT/MOZAMBIQUEEXTN/0,,menuP K:382142~pagePK:141132~piPK:141107~theSitePK:382131,00.html [December 2006]).

19. International Crisis Group, *Somalia's Islamists,* Africa Report 100 (Brussels, 2005).

20. U.S. Department of Defense, "Prepared Testimony of U.S. Secretary of Defense Donald H. Rumsfeld before the Senate Armed Services Committee on Progress in Afghanistan," July 31, 2002 (www.defenselink.mil/speeches/2002/s20020731-secdef.html [December 2006]).

21. World Bank, *World Development Indicators 2006* (Washington, 2006).

22. United Nations Development Program, *Human Development Report 2005* (New York: United Nations, 2005) (http://hdr.undp.org/reports/global/2005/pdf/HDR05_ HDI.pdf [December 2006]).

23. International Crisis Group, *Islamic Terrorism in the Sahel: Fact or Fiction?* Africa Report 92 (Brussels, 2005), 18.

24. Interview with Abass Haidara, the imam of Sankore Mosque in Timbuktu, conducted in London, April 23, 2005.

25. Abu Bakr Naji, *The Management of Savagery: The Most Critical Stage through Which the Umma Will Pass,* trans. William McCants, Combating Terrorism Center, May 23, 2006 (www.ctc.usma.edu/Management_of_Savagery.pdf [December 2006]), 15–16.

26. See Douglas Farah, "Jihadists Now Targeting Africa" (www.douglasfarah.com/archive/2006_06_01_archive.shtml [December 2006]).

27. National Intelligence Council, "The Global Infectious Disease Threat and Its Implications for the United States" (www.dni.gov/nic/PDF_GIF_otherprod/infectious_disease/infectious_diseases.pdf [December 2006]), 5.

28. Information pertaining to animal cases of avian flu is available on the website of the World Organization for Animal Health (http://www.oie.int/eng/info/hebdo/A_DSUM.htm [December 2006]). Information about human cases of avian flu is available through the World Health Organization (www.who.int/csr/disease/avian_influenza/country/cases_table_2006_08_23/en/index.html [December 2006]).

29. World Health Organization, *WHO Ebola Outbreak Chronology* (www.who.int/mediacentre/factsheets/fs103/en/index1.html [December 2006]).

30. Centers for Disease Control and Prevention, *Interim Guidance about Ebola Virus Infection for Airline Flight Crews, Cargo and Cleaning Personnel, and Personnel Interacting with Arriving Passengers* (www.cdc.gov/ncidod/dvrd/spb/mnpages/dispages/ebola/Ebola_airline.pdf [December 2006]).

31. United Nations Development Program, *Human Development Report 2005*, 243, 253.

32. World Health Organization, *WHO Statistics, Core Health Indicators* (www3.who.int/whosis/core/core_select.cfm [December 2006]).

33. World Health Organization, *WHO Weekly Epidemiological Record*, June 23, 2006 (www.who.int/wer/2006/wer8125.pdf [December 2006]).

34. Centers for Disease Control and Prevention, *Outbreak of Rift Valley Fever Saudi Arabia August–November 2000* (www.cdc.gov/mmwr/preview/mmwrhtml/mm4940a1.htm [December 2006]); Centers for Disease Control and Prevention, *Outbreak of Rift Valley Fever Yemen August–October 2000* (www.cdc.gov/mmwr/preview/mmwrhtml/mm4947a3.htm [December 2006]).

35. J. B. McCormick, "A Prospective Study of the Epidemiology and Ecology of Lassa Fever," *Journal of Infectious Diseases* (March 1987): 437–44.

36. World Health Organization, *Weekly Epidemiological Record*, March 11, 2005 (www.who.int/wer/2005/wer8010.pdf [December 2006]).

37. Centers for Disease Control and Prevention, *Morbidity and Mortality Weekly Report*, October 1, 2004 (www.cdc.gov/mmwr/preview/mmwrhtml/mm5338a2.htm [December 2006]).

38. World Health Organization, *WHO Statistics, Core Health Indicators* (www3.who.int/whosis/core/core_select.cfm [December 2006]).

39. Center for Infectious Disease Research and Policy, University of Minnesota, "Dramatic Dengue Spike among U.S. Tropics Travelers" (www.cidrap.umn.edu/cidrap/content/bt/vhf/news/jul0706dengue.html [December 2006]); also see Division of Vector-Borne Infectious Diseases, Centers for Disease Control and Prevention, "Dengue" (www.cdc.gov/ncidod/dvbid/dengue/index.htm#history [December 2006]).

40. UN Food and Agriculture Organization, "Deforestation Continues at an Alarming Rate," FAO Newsroom, November 2005 (www.fao.org/newsroom/en/news/2005/1000127/index.html [December 2006]).

41. World Bank, *World Bank Haiti Country Overview* (http://web.worldbank.org/WBSITE/EXTERNAL/COUNTRIES/LACEXT/HAITIEXTN/0,,content-MDK:20226261~pagePK:141137~piPK:141127~theSitePK:338165,00.html [December 2006]).

42. "Trees in Haiti Fall Victim to Poverty of the People," Associated Press, March 22, 2003.

43. Charles Arthur, "Squalid Excuses," *Guardian,* September 29, 2004.

44. U.S. Agency for International Development, "USAID Congressional Presentation FY 1998: Madagascar; Agency Goal: Protecting the Environment" (www.usaid.gov/pubs/cp98/afr/countries/mg.htm [December 2006]).

45. These figures are derived from country data available through the Food and Agriculture Organization of the United Nations (www.fao.org/forestry/foris/webview/forestry2/index.jsp?siteId=6835&sitetreeId=32085&langId=1&geoId=0 [December 2006]).

46. These data are from Conservation International (www.conservation.org/xp/CIWEB/regions/africa/madagascar.xml [December 2006]).

47. Erin Streff, "Curing Lessons Learned from Plants," *National Geographic News,* March 14, 2001 (http://news.nationalgeographic.com/news/2001/03/0314_plantsheal.html [December 2006]).

48. National Aeronautics and Space Administration, "Earth Observatory, Tropical Deforestation" (http://earthobservatory.nasa.gov/Library/Deforestation/printall.php [December 2006]), 3.

3

Poverty and Violence: An Overview of Recent Research and Implications for Foreign Aid

Edward Miguel

D OZENS OF COUNTRIES around the world have suffered civil conflicts in the
past few decades, with the highest concentration in sub-Saharan Africa.
The humanitarian consequences have been staggering: at least 3 million civilian deaths in the Democratic Republic of the Congo's (the former Zaire) civil
war, and millions of other deaths in Sudan, Rwanda, Sierra Leone, Angola,
Somalia, Uganda, Mozambique, and Liberia, among others. And civil conflict is not just an African problem, as continuing violence in the Middle East
and elsewhere (Colombia, Nepal, and so on) demonstrates.

The direct humanitarian consequences of war for survivors are enormous
in physical insecurity, loss of property, and psychological trauma. There may
also be lasting economic development costs for societies that experience violent civil conflicts. And the international "spillover" effects of conflicts can be
large for neighboring countries faced with refugee flows, lawlessness on their
borders, and the illicit trade in drugs, arms, and minerals that proliferates in
conflict zones. This insecurity has foreign policy implications for the United
States along multiple dimensions.

But what causes this insecurity and what can be done about it? In this
chapter, I first describe recent academic research that finds a strong link leading from poverty to violence in less developed countries. I then lay out some
of the implications of this core finding for public policy and in particular for
the design of foreign aid.

Poverty Leads to Violence in Less Developed Countries

There is increasing evidence of a poverty-violence nexus, at both the macro and micro levels of analysis. This section surveys and critiques recent academic research, highlighting the key findings.

Cross-Country Evidence

There are multiple hypotheses regarding the central causes of violent conflict in less developed countries. Oversimplifying a little, there are two main lines of theorizing. One set of theories stresses the role that political repression, or what are sometimes called "grievance" factors, play in driving conflict. In this view, ethnic groups that experience discrimination should be the most likely to organize armed insurrections against the state, and conflicts should be most likely to erupt in undemocratic states and those with pronounced social divisions.

A second set of theories focuses on economic conditions as paramount, rather than political factors. In other words, in this view, poverty and falling income are the key to sparking civil conflicts. This may be either because poverty breeds armed violence aimed at looting assets and natural resources or, in a variant on the theory advanced by Fearon and Laitin,[1] because poor states simply have limited institutional capacity to repress armed uprisings.

Of course, these two sets of theories are not mutually exclusive; a region that is neglected by the central government in terms of public investment and jobs may become poorer due to its political marginalization, leading to violence. In this case, both perspectives apply.

Turning to the evidence, there is strong support for the poverty-violence nexus. Recent academic research analyzing patterns in real-world data strongly favors the claim that poverty and falling income are the critical drivers of violent conflict in less developed countries. In fact, the poverty-violence link is arguably the most robust finding in the growing research literature investigating the causes of civil wars. But, in a twist, there is far less solid evidence linking political repression to violent conflict.

In a cross-section of countries around the world, Collier and Hoeffler find strong correlations between national income levels and economic growth rates on one hand and the occurrence of civil conflict on the other.[2] They make the theoretical point that joining an armed group becomes more attractive, especially for unemployed young men, when legitimate income-earning options are scarce. There are often numerous lucrative looting, mining, and smuggling opportunities open to armed groups in many developing societies. In contrast, in Collier and Hoeffler's study, the measures of country democracy, income inequality, and ethnic fragmentation are not robustly associated with civil conflict, although they note that research on the role these factors play in civil war's onset remains active.[3]

The key methodological concern with this poverty-violence analysis is the possibility of reverse causation: Could violence be leading to poor economic outcomes in the data, rather than vice versa? Or similarly, could the same institutional factors that lead to political instability and violence also be responsible for poor economic performance?

Rainfall Variation and Civil Conflict

To address these concerns, Miguel, Satyanath, and Sergenti use an alternative statistical approach.[4] With annual country-level data for Africa during the period 1981–99, they studied the effect of droughts (sharp drops in rainfall) on conflict. Droughts lead to large reductions in income in Africa, where the vast majority of the population relies on rain-fed subsistence agriculture. Droughts have the analytical advantage of not being subject to reverse causality; civil war does not cause drought.

Accurate satellite-based rainfall data were utilized to deal with the absence of reliable ground-based rainfall meters in many parts of sub-Saharan Africa. In particular, the Global Precipitation Climatology Project (GPCP) database of monthly rainfall estimates, which stretches back to 1979, was used as a source of data on weather variation.[5] The GPCP data rely on a combination of actual weather station rainfall gauge measures and satellite information on cold cloud cover density (which is closely related to actual precipitation) to derive rainfall estimates.

As far as the mechanics of the rainfall data are concerned, Miguel, Satyanath, and Sergenti have rainfall estimates for each point at which latitude and longitude degree lines cross, at 2.5 degree intervals.[6] Using this data set, they note that Kenya, a medium-sized African country, contains eight rainfall data "nodes," whereas the largest country, Sudan, contains thirty-four nodes. The GPCP rainfall measure at latitude-longitude degree node point p in country i during month m of year t is denoted R_{ipmt}, and the researchers denote the average rainfall across all points p and months m for that year as R_{it}. The principal measure of a rainfall shock is the proportional change in rainfall from the previous year: $(R_{it} - R_{i,t-1})/R_{i,t-1}$. Various alternative measures of rainfall variation were examined—including the sum of squared rainfall deviations across all nodes in a given year, absolute rainfall deviations (from average levels), and absolute rainfall deviations greater than certain threshold levels—but these measures are not as strongly correlated with income growth. Descriptive statistics indicate that there is considerable variation in rainfall in the sample, and this holds both across countries and through time for the same country. Recall that rainfall variability is much greater in sub-Saharan Africa than in tropical regions of Asia or the Americas.[7]

In terms of the civil conflict data, most contributors to the existing literature have worked with, or built on, the Correlates of War (COW) database. However, the lack of transparency and inconsistencies of the COW database are well known. For instance, it is unclear if the COW database uses 1,000 cumulative deaths or 1,000 per year when identifying a civil war. Furthermore, the arbitrary 1,000-death threshold the COW database uses to identify a civil war has the danger of excluding conflicts that may be major for smaller countries, including many African countries.

Miguel, Satyanath, and Sergenti instead used the Armed Conflict database developed by the International Peace Research Institute of Oslo and the University of Uppsala (referred to as PRIO/Uppsala). The PRIO/Uppsala database is more transparent in its construction than COW, and also, uniquely, records all conflicts with a threshold of 25 battle deaths per year, in addition to classifying conflicts by the standard 1,000-death threshold, thus including more small conflicts in the analysis. An armed conflict is defined in the PRIO/Uppsala database as follows: "a contested incompatibility which concerns government and/or territory where the use of armed force between two parties, of which at least one is the government of a state, results in at least 25 battle-related deaths."[8] The database is careful to focus only on politically motivated violence.

Note that, like other cross-country civil war data sets, PRIO/Uppsala unfortunately does not include conflict information at the subnational level; nor does it provide the exact number of conflict deaths, and this by necessity limits certain aspects of the analysis. The analysis has other limitations. First, the above definition of conflict means that Miguel, Satyanath, and Sergenti do not capture many important types of organized violence in sub-Saharan Africa that do not directly involve the state—for instance, clashes among pastoralist groups in northern Kenya—that are of considerable research interest in their own right. Finally, though the PRIO/Uppsala database also includes detailed information on conflicts between countries, Miguel, Satyanath, and Sergenti focus exclusively on civil wars.

The civil conflict indicator variable takes on a value of 1 for all country-year observations with a civil conflict in progress with at least 25 battle deaths per year (or 1,000 battle deaths, in some specifications), and other observations are zeros. Civil conflict was remarkably widespread in sub-Saharan Africa during the period 1981–99; there was civil conflict in fully 27 percent of all country-year observations, according to the PRIO/Uppsala 25-annual-battle-deaths definition; 17 percent according to the PRIO/Uppsala 1,000-deaths definition; and 24 percent under the Fearon and Laitin definition, using a 1,000-death threshold. Thirty-eight separate civil conflicts began during the sample period 1981–99—not including conflicts that were already ongoing in 1981—and twenty-seven ended, at least temporarily.

The first step in the statistical analysis by Miguel, Satyanath, and Sergenti, and what economists call the "first-stage regression," is determining the relationship between rainfall shocks and economic growth. This relationship is strongly positive; current rainfall growth and lagged rainfall growth are both significantly related to income growth at over 95 percent confidence, and this relationship is robust to the inclusion of country controls and fixed effects. As expected, positive rainfall growth typically leads to better agricultural production because most of sub-Saharan Africa lies within the semiarid tropics and is prone to drought.

The next step is to determine how rainfall itself directly affects the likelihood of civil conflict, the "reduced form relationship" in econometric parlance. Drops in rainfall are associated with significantly more conflict, with a point estimate of –0.122 (standard error 0.052) on lagged rainfall growth.[9] In the case of major conflicts, those involving more than 1,000 deaths a year, coefficient estimates on both current and lagged growth are statistically significant at 95 percent confidence. This is strong evidence that better rainfall makes conflict much less likely in Africa.

These two analyses are then combined into what economists call "instrumental variables" (IV) estimation, to back out the effect of economic growth on conflict, utilizing only the variation in income induced by rainfall shocks and thus avoiding the reverse causality problem. Because Miguel, Satyanath, and Sergenti have instrumented for economic growth, they make the causal assertion that the incidence of civil wars in sub-Saharan Africa is influenced by economic shocks.

The researchers discovered that economic shocks have an even more dramatic impact on civil war incidence than had been previously recognized. The size of the estimated impact of lagged economic growth on conflict is huge; focusing on the IV regression with country fixed-effect controls, they determined the point estimate indicates that a 1 percentage point decline in gross domestic product increases the likelihood of civil conflict by more than

2 percentage points. This implies that a drop in per capita income due to drought of 5 percent in one year increases the likelihood of a civil conflict in the following year by nearly half, a very large effect. This analysis highlights the key role that income volatility has played in generating armed violence.

Echoing Collier and Hoeffler, Miguel, Satyanath, and Sergenti do not find any meaningful direct effect of democratic freedoms or ethnic fragmentation on conflict outbreaks. They also find that the impact of economic growth shocks on the incidence of major conflicts is remarkably—and perhaps surprisingly—similar for African countries across a wide range of institutional, political, social, and economic characteristics. There are good theoretical reasons to expect to find strong effects; for instance, given an adverse economic growth shock, countries with stronger democratic institutions (and similarly, wealthier countries) may be better able to negotiate compromises among social groups to avert unrest, whereas such negotiations may more often break down in ethnically or religiously fragmented societies.

However, the relationship between economic growth shocks and conflict is similar for countries with different levels of democratic freedoms or per capita income levels in 1979. In other words, undemocratic African countries hit by negative income shocks are just as prone to civil conflict as relatively democratic countries, suggesting that even the more democratic states in Africa typically lack the institutional capability to adequately respond to negative economic shocks and avert conflict.

Economic growth shocks also do not have a differential impact in more ethnically diverse countries, in oil-producing countries, or in mountainous countries. There is no significant difference in the effect of economic growth on conflict across former British colonies, former French colonies, and former colonies of other countries; by African subregion (Central, East, Southern, and West Africa); for countries with socialist political regimes at the start of the sample period; by religious fractionalization, or several other social fractionalization measures; by population density; for a range of measures of democracy, political competition, regulation of political participation, and constitutional constraints on executive power (from the Polity IV data set); for other political institutional measures, including the degree of federalism and government checks and balances (from the World Bank Database of Political Institutions); and for political and civil freedom (from Freedom House).

The most obvious reading of these findings is that economic factors trump all others in causing African civil conflicts, and that institutional and political characteristics have much less of an impact.

Additional Evidence on the Poverty-Violence Nexus

This core relationship running from poverty to violence also holds at lower levels of analysis. In Nepal, a higher poverty rate at the district level is associated with significantly more civil war deaths, in the ongoing Maoist insurgency there.[10] Again, local measures of social divisions (for example, ethnic and caste diversity) are not correlated with district violence.

The existence of easily lootable resources in the context of a bitterly poor society can drive violence. Bellows and Miguel find significantly more armed clashes in Sierra Leone chiefdoms with greater diamond wealth, and less fighting in areas without these resources.[11] Diamonds played a key role in financing armed factions there and were a magnet for violence. Consistent with the cross-country studies mentioned above, there is a consensus both within Sierra Leone and in the academic literature that the civil war there was not predominantly an "ethnic conflict."

Broader continentwide trends are also consistent with the poverty-violence nexus view, although statistical analysis at this level of aggregation is by necessity more speculative. The past five years have seen a gradual reduction in the overall number of civil conflicts in Africa, with the end of several protracted civil wars (in Angola, Liberia, and Sierra Leone). Improving economic conditions are likely to be playing some role in this decrease; average per capita income growth in sub-Saharan Africa as a whole has been positive for the first time since the 1970s, driven in part by rising global commodity prices. The bottom line is that boosting living standards may be the most effective way to reduce civil conflict in Africa—and elsewhere—in the long run.

Implications for Foreign Aid: Rapid Conflict Prevention Support

Most foreign aid currently focuses on long-run investments in education, health, and infrastructure. To the extent that foreign aid promotes long-run economic growth—an issue that remains contested—this assistance would reduce civil conflict in the long run by making recipient countries richer. These more prosperous citizens should then find joining an armed insurgency less attractive than legitimate economic activities.

However, most foreign aid does little to deal with the immediate triggers of civil conflict in the short run. One implication of the research discussed above is that a larger share of foreign aid should also aim to eliminate the sharp income fluctuations that generate support for armed groups in less developed countries. Poor countries have always had much more volatile per capita income than wealthy countries for a variety of reasons, including their dependence on rain-fed agriculture and on a limited number of volatile export commodities. When the rains fail one year, or there is a collapse in the world market price for a key export, sharp income contractions are common. sub-Saharan African countries are particularly notorious for their highly volatile national incomes.

One possible approach is for more foreign aid to explicitly play an *insurance* role. I call this new type of aid Rapid Conflict Prevention Support (RCPS). RCPS aid would target countries experiencing temporary income drops due to poor weather or adverse commodity price movements, both of which are easily monitored by aid donors (using existing databases such as the Famine Early Warning System for Africa). There would also be little incentive for governments to "game" the system to receive such financing. These two factors—weather and global commodity prices—are largely out of the control of governments, maintaining government incentives for responsible economic policy.

This form of donor support would temporarily bolster local economic conditions at key junctures, when the risk of social instability is high. RCPS could augment rather than replace traditional forms of foreign aid. When objective underlying local economic factors improve—for example, rains improve the next year, or world coffee prices rebound—this RCPS aid to the government could quickly be reduced, as the state's own revenues pick up. Targeting RCPS aid toward the social groups most likely to participate in armed violence—for example, in temporary job creation for unemployed young men in a dissident region—might be most effective in preventing armed conflicts from occurring in conflict-prone countries and regions. Another attractive option in rural areas would be for aid to serve as crop insurance for farmers.

Several rural insurance programs already exist in the more economically successful African countries, most notably a program that provides drought assistance to farmers in Botswana, and these could serve as "models" for other economies. Drought is a frequent visitor to Botswana, as in much of the semiarid tropics. To deal with this problem, the government has for decades implemented a multifaceted policy called the Drought Relief Program (DRP).[12] DRP consists of direct income support for rural households in years when the rains fail, including public works employment programs as well as food aid for the most vulnerable. The government takes drought seriously; for instance, it is estimated that up to 60 percent of rural Botswanans received some DRP assistance during the severe mid-1980s drought. In those difficult years, DRP helped to reduce rural poverty and income inequality, preserving social stability.

Many details of RCPS design and implementation still need to be worked out, and these might vary depending on the needs and institutions of the recipient country. RCPS would ideally not be a "one-size-fits-all" program, and it could differ from the Botswanan model. For example, in some settings, channeling RCPS assistance through the government could be the most timely and cost-effective approach, whereas in other cases nongovernmental organizations would be preferred. Similarly, the decision whether to target assistance to unemployed urban workers versus farmers will depend on local social conditions.

Other types of foreign aid are related to the RCPS I have briefly described, but they differ in key ways.[13] Humanitarian aid also serves as a form of insurance for poor countries suffering from major natural calamities and wars. But, crucially, this aid is provided by the international community *after* a conflict has already broken out. RCPS would identify those countries most likely to suffer from conflict in the near future and would increase foreign flows *before* any violence erupts. In this sense, RCPS aid can also be seen as a cost-effective investment in future peace and security, as "prevention" rather than a costly "cure."

Some International Monetary Fund lending also can serve as insurance, at least in theory—for example, the Compensatory and Contingency Financing Facility (CCFF) and the new Exogenous Shocks Facility. However, neither of these is currently linked to objective measures of conflict risk, and the CCFF has historically been very rarely used.[14] The Fund's conditionality also eliminates many of the most conflict-prone countries from consideration for lending through these financing facilities.

Foreign aid of course has multiple goals, including long-run economic and institutional development as well as donors' political objectives. But, arguably, too little of this aid is currently structured with the goal of preventing armed civil conflicts. Such conflicts often last for many years, have claimed millions of lives, and have created failed-state havens for international criminals and terrorists. If RCPS could reduce the chance of a conflict breaking out, even slightly, would it not be worth it?

Notes

1. James Fearon and David Laitin, "Ethnicity, Insurgency and Civil War," *American Political Science Review* 97, no. 1 (2003): 75–90.

2. Paul Collier and Anke Hoeffler, "On the Incidence of Civil War in Africa," *Journal of Conflict Resolution* 46, no. 1 (2002): 13–28.

3. As discussed by Håvard Hegre and Nicholas Sambanis, "Sensitivity Analysis of Empirical Results on Civil War Onset," *Journal of Conflict Resolution* 50, no. 4 (2006): 508–35.

4. Edward Miguel, Shanker Satyanath, and Ernest Sergenti, "Economic Shocks and Civil Conflict: An Instrumental Variables Approach," *Journal of Political Economy* 112, no. 4 (2004): 725–53.

5. The GPCP data are publicly available at http://orbit-net.nesdis.noaa.gov/arad/gpcp/.

6. No degree grid node fell within the national boundaries for five small African countries—Burundi, Djibouti, Gambia, Guinea-Bissau, and Rwanda—so in these cases we assigned them rainfall measures from the nearest node.

7. David E. Bloom and Jeffrey D. Sachs, "Geography, Demography, and Economic Growth in Africa," *Brookings Papers on Economic Activity* 2 (1998): 222.

8. Refer to the PRIO website (www.prio.no/cwp/ArmedConflict) or the University of Uppsala website (www.pcr.uu.se). A detailed description of the criteria used to code civil wars is provided in Nils Petter Gleditsch, Peter Wallensteen, Mikael Eriksson, Margareta Sollenberg, and Håvard Strand, "Armed Conflict 1946–2001: A New Dataset," *Journal of Peace Research* 39, no. 5 (2002): 615–37.

9. The regression details can be found in Miguel, Satyanath, and Sergenti, "Economic Shocks and Civil Conflict."

10. Quy-Toan Do and Iyer Lakshmi, "An Empirical Analysis of Civil Conflict in Nepal," Institute of Governmental Studies, University of California, Berkeley, WP2006'14 (2006).

11. John Bellows and Edward Miguel, "War and Local Collective Action in Sierra Leone," unpublished working paper, University of California, Berkeley, 2006.

12. For further discussion, refer to Theodore Valentine, "Drought, Transfers, Entitlements and Income Distribution: The Botswana Experience," *World Development* 21, no. 1 (1993): 109–26.

13. The most closely related discussion of foreign aid and conflict prevention, to my knowledge, is Paul Collier and Anke Hoeffler, "Aid, Policy and Peace: Reducing the Risks of Civil Conflict," *Defense and Peace Economics* 13, no. 6 (2002): 435–50. They also make the claim that an increase in foreign aid is likely to reduce civil conflict risk, and they empirically demonstrate some modest reductions in conflict for aid recipients, working through the channel of faster economic growth. Yet they study the effect of existing foreign aid instruments on conflict, rather than aid with the monitoring mechanisms, timing, and targeting in the RCPS proposal.

14. The history of the Compensatory and Contingency Financing Facility is discussed in International Monetary Fund, "Buffer Stock Financing Facility (BSFF): Preliminary Considerations," Policy Development and Review Department in consultation with other departments, December 9, 1999; and International Monetary Fund, "Review of the Compensatory and Contingency Financing Facility (CCFF)," Policy Development and Review Department in consultation with other departments, December 9, 1999.

4

Demography, Environment, and Civil Strife

Colin H. Kahl

AT BOTH THE global and local levels, natural resource depletion and environmental degradation result from the interactions among extreme wealth, population pressures, and extreme poverty. The material-intensive and pollution-laden consumption habits and production activities of high-income countries are responsible for most of the world's greenhouse gases, solid and hazardous waste, and other environmental pollution. High-income countries also generate a disproportionate amount of the global demand for fossil fuels, nonfuel minerals, grain, meat, fish, tropical hardwoods, and products from endangered species.[1]

Poverty and inequality within developing countries, especially those with rapidly growing populations, also places burdens on the environment. Impoverished individuals frequently live in the most fragile ecological areas and are often driven to overexploit croplands, pastures, forests, fisheries, and water resources in order to eke out a living. Many have been forced to migrate to marginal areas due to overcrowding on better land. In the past fifty years, the number of people living on fragile land in developing countries has doubled to 1.3 billion, and rural population growth remains higher than average in countries with 30 percent or more of their population living on fragile land. Fragile ecological areas, which represent 73 percent of the Earth's land surface, have a very limited ability to sustain high population densities and are particularly vulnerable to degradation, erosion, flooding, fires, landslides, and climatic change.[2]

The relationship between the environment and poverty runs both ways. Poverty can contribute to environmental degradation, which in turn worsens poverty, and so on. Today, nearly half the world's population lives on less than $2 a day, and more than 1 billion people eke out a living on less than $1 a day. The absolute number of people living on less than $1 a day has actually fallen from 1.5 to 1.1 billion over the past twenty years, even as the world's population has expanded by 1.6 billion, but most of these gains have occurred in just two countries: China and India. In many other parts of the developing world, poverty remains a seemingly intractable problem. And in some regions, especially sub-Saharan Africa, the absolute number of extremely impoverished individuals has more than doubled since the early 1980s. Today, more than 1.3 billion people depend on agriculture, forests, and fisheries for their livelihoods. This represents around half of total global employment. Consequently, when the local environment is degraded and resource competition becomes more acute, it can have significant implications for the economic survival of entire communities.[3]

Numerous signs suggest that the combined effects of unsustainable consumption, population growth, and extreme poverty are taking their toll on the environment. To take one example, the World Wildlife Fund (WWF) has recently calculated humanity's "ecological footprint" by comparing renewable resource consumption to an estimate of nature's biological productive capacity. A country's ecological footprint represents the total area (measured in standardized global hectares of biologically productive land and water) required to produce the renewable resources consumed and to assimilate the wastes generated by human activities. All told, the global footprint in 1999 amounted to 13.7 billion biologically productive hectares, exceeding the 11.4 billion hectares estimated to exist by about 20 percent. Moreover, in the decades ahead as economic globalization accelerates, the human population continues to expand (with the fastest rates of growth occurring in the world's least developed nations), and the effects of human-induced climate change become more pronounced, the strain on the natural environment is likely to worsen.[4]

What are the implications of these trends for international security? Though there is scant evidence that population and environmental pressure produce armed clashes *between* countries (with the partial exception of conflicts over oil and water), a growing body of scholarship has linked these factors to violence *within* countries. Some see demographically and environmentally induced scarcity as a major source of civil strife, while others argue that a local abundance of valuable natural resources produces greater dangers.

The Demography–Environment–Civil Strife Connection

Since the early 1990s, a number of academics and international security specialists have argued that demographic and environmental pressures pose significant threats to political stability in developing countries. Initially, this discussion was dominated by neo-Malthusians, but more recently a number of scholars working within the tradition of neoclassical economics have entered the fray.

Deprivation and Failed States

Neo-Malthusians argue that rapid population growth, environmental degradation, resource depletion, and unequal resource access combine to exacerbate poverty and income inequality in many of the world's least developed countries. The resulting rise in absolute and relative deprivation translates into grievances, increasing the risks of rebellion and societal conflict.[5]

More recent work in this tradition acknowledges that deprivation by itself is rarely sufficient to produce large-scale organized violence, because the poor often lack the capabilities to rebel, especially in the context of a strong state. Therefore, neo-Malthusians contend that population and environmental pressures are most likely to contribute to internal wars when demographic and environmental pressures also weaken state authority, thereby opening "political space" for violence to occur.[6]

Demographic and environmental stress can undermine state authority in a number of ways. As population and environmental challenges mount, so will the demands placed on the state from suffering segments of the economy and marginalized individuals. Demands may include calls for costly development projects, such as hydroelectric dams, canals, and irrigation systems; subsidies for fertilizer and other agricultural inputs; and urban demands for employment, housing, schools, sanitation, energy, and lower food prices. These demands increase fiscal strains and thus erode a state's administrative capacity by requiring budgetary trade-offs. A state's legitimacy may also be cast into doubt if individuals and groups come to blame the government for their plight. Population growth, environmental degradation, and resource depletion can also undermine overall economic productivity, thereby reducing the revenue available to local and central governments at the very time that rising demands require greater expenditures.[7] Research suggests that these dynamics have historically contributed to civil strife in the state of Chiapas in Mexico, El Salvador, the Philippines, Somalia, and elsewhere.[8]

In addition to increasing the risks of violent rebellion from below, state weakness and rising social grievances emanating from demographic and environmental stress can sometimes encourage political elites themselves to instigate civil strife in an effort to cling to power. Ethnic clashes in Kenya in the early 1990s illustrate this pathway to violence. During the 1980s, population growth averaging 3.4 percent a year combined with soil erosion, desertification, and unequal land access to create an extreme scarcity of arable land, escalating economic marginalization in rural areas, and substantial rural-to-urban migration. As the population of Nairobi and Kenya's other urban centers soared, and related social and economic problems worsened, pressure mounted on President Daniel arap Moi's regime to forsake the KANU Party's monopoly on rule and allow multiparty elections. In response to this threat, Moi and many of his close associates set out to discredit the democratization process and consolidate their control over the valuable and fertile Rift Valley by orchestrating a series of tribal clashes that left 1,500 dead and hundreds of thousands homeless. To implement this strategy, KANU elites capitalized on and manipulated a set of demographically, environmentally, and historically rooted land grievances between pastoral groups and farming communities.[9] Similar dynamics have contributed to violent conflicts in Darfur (Sudan), Rwanda, and Zimbabwe.[10]

Honey Pots and the Resource Curse

Neoclassical economists advance a set of claims that, on the surface at least, appear to turn neo-Malthusian arguments on their head. Resource abundance, rather than scarcity, is argued to be the bigger threat to political instability.

One claim centers on so-called honey pot effects. According to this view, abundant supplies of valuable local resources create incentives for rebel groups to form and fight to capture them. This can spawn attempts by regional warlords and rebel organizations to cleave off resource-rich territories or violently hijack the state. Once seized, control over valuable natural resources fuels conflict escalation by allowing the parties to purchase weaponry and mobilize potential recruits.[11] Recent conflicts fueled by diamonds and other precious minerals in Sierra Leone and the Democratic Republic of the Congo demonstrate the honey pot effect in action.

Some neoclassical economists argue that natural resource abundance also produces weak states via a set of developmental pathologies known collectively as the resource curse. Economically, abundant natural resources are said to contribute to economic stagnation over the long run through a number of crowding-out effects sometimes referred to as "Dutch disease." When capital and labor focus on booming natural resource sectors, they are drawn away from other sectors of the economy, increasing their production costs. These economic distortions slow the maturity of non-resource-tradable sectors, harm their competitiveness, and thereby inhibit the kinds of economic diversification, especially an early period of labor-intensive manufacturing, that many neoclassical economists suggest is vital for long-term growth. It is also argued that overreliance on exports of minimally processed natural resources makes countries vulnerable to declining terms of trade and the highly volatile nature of international commodities markets. In the absence of a diverse array of exports, especially of manufactured goods that tend to have more stable prices, resource-rich countries are prone to dramatic economic shocks when prices for primary commodities inevitably crash.[12]

Beyond the economic distortions created by local resource abundance, there is also a political dimension to the resource curse. The most common political argument focuses on problems associated with "rentier states"; these states, which accrue a significant amount of revenue from natural resource exports they directly control, are prone to developing corrupt, narrowly based authoritarian or quasi-democratic governing institutions. When states capture enormous rents from natural resources, they face far fewer incentives to bargain away greater economic and political accountability to the populace in exchange for broader rights of taxation. Instead, natural resource wealth can be used to maintain rule through patronage networks and outright coercion. The institutional makeup of rentier states therefore reduces the prospects for broad-based, benevolent economic and political reform, weakening the state over the long term and generating substantial societal grievances.[13] These conditions are ripe for violent revolt.[14]

There appears to be strong cross-national evidence for the developmental problems associated with the resource curse. Statistical analyses suggest that countries that are highly dependent on primary commodity exports have, on average, lower rates of economic growth and more unequal distributions of income.[15] Underdevelopment and poor governance, in turn, can generate grievances and open political space for organized violence. For example, many oil-exporting countries, including Algeria, Angola, Ecuador, Indonesia, Iraq, and Nigeria, have historically been prone to authoritarianism, corruption, periodic social protests, and violence.[16] Recently, some have also expressed fears that Dutch disease and rentier-state pathologies could pose significant threats to the future stability of post-Saddam Iraq. If an equitable system is not established to manage and distribute the country's oil wealth among its various regions and religious and ethnic communities, these forces could have a corrupting influence on future political institutions, put any new government's legitimacy at risk, and spur bloody competition among Shiites, Sunnis, Kurds, and Turkmen.

Evaluating the Debate

Neo-Malthusians and neoclassical economists seem to advance polar-opposite views. The former see too few natural resources as the problem, while the latter see too many resources as the curse. Thus, while neo-Malthusians would be concerned about the potentially destabilizing effects of demographic, economic, and environmental trends, especially in the world's least developed countries, neoclassical economists might argue that rising demographic and environmental pressures will create incentives for countries to diversify their economies away from natural resource dependence, ultimately making them more prosperous and stable. Upon deeper reflection, however, the arguments advanced are not as incompatible as they first appear.

Scarcity versus Abundance

Natural resource scarcity and abundance as conceptualized by neo-Malthusians and neoclassical economists are not opposites; they can, and often do, both exist at the same time at different levels of analysis. The vast majority of troublesome resources discussed by neoclassical economists (oil, gemstones, valuable metals, timber, and so on) are abundant locally but scarce globally, something neo-Malthusians are careful to point out.[17] Indeed, it is the global scarcity of these resources that makes them so valuable and thus such huge prizes to seize through violence.

Furthermore, abundance of one resource can produce scarcity of another. The extraction and production activities centered on locally abundant (and usually nonrenewable) resources can lead to environmental degradation and scarcities of *other* (usually renewable) resources, and the synergy may lead to violent conflict. In Nigeria, for example, revenue streams from the oil-rich Niger Delta have historically filled the coffers of a small minority and propped up a series of repressive regimes. Throughout the 1990s, inequities, environmental degradation, pollution, and health problems stemming from the oil industry generated substantial grievances among local communities in the Niger Delta, including the Ogoni people. In the mid-1990s, the military dictatorship in Nigeria responded to Ogoni protests with repression and the instigation of interethnic violence.[18]

Finally, abundance and scarcity combine to pose development challenges for resource-dependent countries. In many respects, neo-Malthusians and neoclassical economists speak past each other because they ignore the notions of time and sequence that are implicit in their analyses. To see how both types of logic may operate and actually reinforce one another, consider three idealized temporal stages in a country whose economy is dependent on local supplies of natural resources: (1) initial abundance; (2) emerging scarcity; and (3) the time at which exploitation of the scarce local resource is no longer economically viable, forcing diversification and a search for alternative supplies and substitutes. Neo-Malthusians and neoclassical economists should *both* agree that the second phase holds the highest risk of internal war.

The logic of the honey pot effect, for example, applies much more during a time of emerging scarcity. After all, when natural resources are consumed or degraded at unsustainable rates, their value increases and rival social groups confront greater incentives to seize them. The renewal of civil war in Sudan in 1983 provides a clear example here. By the end of the 1970s, environmental stress in northern Sudan, stemming in large part from mechanized farming, increased the value of water, land, and oil resources in the south. Northern elites, acting in support of allied northern mechanized farm owners, pushed south to capture these resources. This posed an enormous threat to the economic and physical survival of southerners, encouraging them to restart the war against the north. As the war raged on, oil exports became central to the north's ability to finance its campaign, encouraging it to seize and exploit oil deposits deeper and deeper into the south.[19]

Moreover, if development is viewed as a sequence of temporal stages, a good case can also be made that the developmental pathologies of the resource curse and those emerging from rapid population growth, environmental degradation, and resource scarcity can all occur and interact with one another within the same country over time. During stage 1, when resources are abundant, a country may become highly dependent on these resources and elements of Dutch disease and rentier state politics may take hold. Then, during stage 2, demographic and environmental pressures may produce growing scarcities and undermine economic and political stability *precisely because* the country developed such a strong dependence on exporting natural resources in the first place. Finally, at stage 3, scarcity and economic crisis may force the government and the private sector to promote diversification as a means of resuscitating growth. This hypothetical sequence suggests that neoclassical theorists tend to focus on the logic involved in the leaps between these temporal stages without sufficiently recognizing the risks of transitional violence during the middle stage emphasized by neo-Malthusians.

By ignoring transitional dangers, neoclassical economists miss important contributors to civil strife. The experience of the world's poorest countries suggests that many are currently stuck in stage 2, where high dependence on natural resources, rapid population growth, environmental degradation, and emerging scarcity conspire to threaten political stability.

Different Resources, Different Risks

Different types of natural resources are likely to be implicated in different types of conflict. In fact, a close look at the conflict claims advanced by neo-Malthusians and neoclassical economists reveals that they are generally not talking about the same resources.

The broad grievance-based scenarios identified by neo-Malthusians are most likely when international demand, local population dynamics, unsustainable extraction practices, and unequal resource access interact to produce environmental degradation and emerging scarcities of *renewable* resources. Agriculture, forestry, and fishing contribute much more to employment than capital-intensive nonrenewable resource sectors. Moreover, access to arable land (or inexpensive food) and freshwater is vital to extremely poor individuals throughout the developing world. Degradation, depletion, and/or maldistributions of these resources can therefore directly implicate the survival of large numbers of people in rural areas in ways that nonrenewables usually do not. Of course, in some instances, the extraction of nonrenewable resources causes degradation, depletion, or unequal distributions of renewable ones, but even here it is the impact on the surrounding renewable resource base that is likely to have the widest direct effect on the quality of life and related grievances.

Nonrenewable resources are much more likely to be implicated in the conflict scenarios outlined by neoclassical economists. Nonrenewable resources are likely to be central to violent conflicts in which natural resources themselves are the main prize to be captured, as opposed to conflicts emanating from the more diffuse social and economic effects of environmental degradation and renewable resource scarcity. According to the honey pot logic, the incentive and capability to capture nonrenewable resources is especially high because mineral resources tend to be much more valuable per unit of volume, geographically concentrated, and easily tradable than most renewable resources. These features make nonrenewable resources considerably more "lootable."[20] It should come as no surprise, therefore, that the vast majority of honey pot–driven conflicts revolve around oil, diamonds, and other valuable minerals.

The economic and political components of the resource curse also apply much more to countries dependent on the export of nonrenewable resources. Here, several characteristics distinguish mineral-dependent economies and polities from countries dependent on renewables (again, with the partial exception of timber). Mineral-exporting countries tend to be economically dependent on a single resource. Consequently, their economies tend to be especially sensitive to price volatility.[21] Furthermore, mining countries are typically dependent on resources that generate extraordinary rents. This is especially true of oil, but is also the case with other minerals.

States in the developing world also exercise sole ownership rights over sub-soil assets and, often, public forestlands. This means that the export revenue from these resources is not mediated through domestic private actors but instead accrues directly to the state and allied firms. This differs dramatically from the situation in most countries dependent on exports of agriculture because these resources tend to be privately owned (even if sometimes highly concentrated). Thus, because government officials have the ability to extract and control an unusually high income from nonrenewables, the pathologies of rentier state politics are likely to be much more acute than in countries dependent on most renewable resources.[22]

The Importance of Political Institutions

Demographic and environmental pressures are rarely if ever sufficient to pro-duce conflict; many countries experience these pressures yet avoid civil strife. Neo-Malthusians and neoclassical economists generally agree that demo-graphically and environmentally induced civil wars are most likely in coun-tries with weak governments and authoritarian political institutions.

As noted above, strong states are typically able to prevent, deter, or repress large-scale organized violence initiated by potential challengers. Strong states are also less vulnerable to conflicts initiated by state elites themselves because elites generally feel more secure and are able to advance their interests with-out risking societywide warfare. Beyond the strength of the state, the charac-ter of a country's governing institutions also matters. Consolidated democra-cies are unlikely candidates for civil war and are less vulnerable to widespread upheaval during times of crisis. Democracies normally enjoy greater system legitimacy than authoritarian states and are better able to channel grievances into the normal political process. Democratic institutions also increase the transparency of political decisions and place constraints on executive authority, limiting the ability of state elites to instigate violence.[23]

Quantitative studies suggest that many consolidated authoritarian states also avoid civil war. Nevertheless, their stability typically relies on a high degree of coercive power and patronage, and these governments often generate substantial antistate grievances, especially among excluded social groups. Consequently, these states are vulnerable to rapid collapse and civil war during times of crisis or regime transition.[24]

All told, when the strength of the state and the character of its political institutions are taken into consideration, it becomes clear that some political contexts are especially vulnerable to demographically and environmentally induced violence. The natural resource–civil strife connection is likely to be particularly tight when population growth, environmental degradation, resource scarcity, and/or the pathologies of the resource curse contribute to state weakness and authoritarian institutions, or when demographically and environmentally induced grievances and honey pot effects occur in the context of states that are already weak and narrow or undergoing rapid regime transition.

Implications for the Future

During the next half century, the UN medium projection estimates that the world's population will increase from 6.5 billion in 2005 to 9.1 billion in 2050. Population growth is projected to slow across the board, but differential growth rates between rich and poor countries are expected to persist. Indeed, by 2050 the population of the high-income countries is expected to be in the midst of a twenty-year *decline*. In contrast, the population of the least developed countries is projected to more than double from 800 million in 2005 to 1.7 billion by 2050. In the rest of the developing world, the population is expected to increase from 4.5 to 6.1 billion over this period.[25]

Economic growth and consumption are also projected to increase in the decades ahead, spurred on by continued economic globalization. The World Bank projects growth in global income of 3 percent a year over the next fifty years, suggesting a fourfold rise in global gross domestic product (to a total of $140 trillion) by midcentury. Historically, higher income is associated with higher levels of consumption, although the relationship is usually nonlinear.[26]

Although it is impossible to predict the future of any complex system, let alone a future based on the intersection of several complex systems (demographic, economic, political, and environmental), some have offered possible scenarios. The WWF has projected humanity's ecological footprint forward from 2000 to 2050 by combining UN population growth estimates, Intergovernmental Panel on Climate Change estimates of future carbon dioxide emissions, and UN Food and Agriculture Organization estimates of trends in the consumption of agriculture products (crops, meat, and dairy), forest products (including fuelwood), and fish and seafood. According to this projection, a population of 9 billion in 2050 will require 1.8 to 2.2 Earth-sized planets to sustain its total consumption of crops, meat, fish, and wood, and to hold carbon dioxide levels constant in the atmosphere. Whether this scenario comes about obviously depends on future consumption habits and available technology. Rapid advances in technology that provide for significant improvements in resource efficiency, for example, could allow for long-term sustainability and continued advances in human welfare; however, without significant technological changes, the projected consumption would become unsustainable.[27]

Consumption will likely drive global patterns of resource depletion and pollution, but population growth and poverty will continue to have an important impact at the local level. Even as globalization raises the living standards of some countries and peoples, pockets of extreme poverty and yawning inequalities are likely to persist, placing their own strains on the environment. Current projections suggest that millions of people in the developing world will continue to rely on overcrowded and ecologically fragile lands where there is a real danger of becoming trapped in a vicious cycle of poverty and environmental decline. This is likely to generate substantial challenges for both human welfare and political stability.

Notes

1. World Bank, *World Development Report 2003: Sustainable Development in a Dynamic World* (Oxford University Press, 2003), 118; Worldwatch Institute, *Vital Signs 2003* (New York: W. W. Norton, 2003): 17; World Resources Institute, *World Resources 2000–2001* (Oxford: Elsevier Science, 2000), 26–27.

2. World Bank, *World Development Indicators* (Washington, 2003), 118; World Bank, *World Development Report 2003,* 7–8, 60–67; Worldwatch Institute, *Vital Signs 2003,* 17.

3. World Resources Institute, *World Resources* (Washington, 2005).

4. Mathis Wackernagel and others, "Tracking the Ecological Overshoot of the Human Economy," *Proceedings of the National Academy of Sciences* 99, no. 14 (2002): 9266–71; World Wildlife Fund, *Living Planet Report 2002* (Gland, Switzerland, 2002).

5. Norman Myers, *Ultimate Security: The Environmental Basis of Political Stability* (New York: W. W. Norton, 1993); also see Jessica Tuchman Matthews, "Redefining Security," *Foreign Affairs,* Spring 1989, 162–77.

6. Jack A. Goldstone, *Revolution and Rebellion in the Early Modern World* (University of California Press, 1991); Jack A. Goldstone, "Population Growth and Revolutionary Crises," in *Theorizing Revolutions,* ed. John Foran (London: Routledge, 1997), 102–20; Jack A. Goldstone, "How Demographic Change Can Lead to Violent Conflict," *Journal of International Affairs* 56, no. 1 (2002): 3–24; Thomas F. Homer-Dixon, "On the Threshold: Environmental Changes as Causes of Acute Conflict," *International Security* 16, no. 2 (1991): 76–116; Thomas F. Homer-Dixon, "Environmental Scarcities and Violent Conflict: Evidence from Cases," *International Security* 19, no. 1 (1994): 4–40; Thomas F. Homer-Dixon, *Environment, Scarcity, and Violence* (Princeton University Press, 1999); Colin H. Kahl, *States, Scarcity, and Civil Strife in the Developing World* (Princeton University Press, 2006). Also see Robert D. Kaplan, "The Coming Anarchy," *Atlantic Monthly,* February 1994, 44–76.

7. Homer-Dixon, "Environmental Scarcities and Violent Conflict," 25–26; Kahl, *States, Scarcity, and Civil Strife,* 40–44.

8. Homer-Dixon, *Environment, Scarcity, and Violence,* 142–47; Kahl, *States, Scarcity, and Civil Strife,* chaps. 3, 6; Myers, *Ultimate Security,* 122–29.

9. Colin H. Kahl, "Population Growth, Environmental Degradation, and State-Sponsored Violence: The Case of Kenya, 1991–1993," *International Security* 23, no. 2 (1998): 80–119; Kahl, *States, Scarcity, and Civil Strife,* chap. 4.

10. Kahl, *States, Scarcity, and Civil Strife,* chap. 6.

11. Paul Collier and Anke Hoeffler, "Greed and Grievance in Civil War," World Bank, October 21, 2001; World Bank, *World Development Indicators* (Washington, 2003); Indra de Soysa, "The Resource Curse: Are Civil Wars Driven by Rapacity or Paucity?" in *Greed and Grievance: Economic Agendas in Civil Wars,* ed. Mats Berdal and David M. Malone (Boulder, Colo.: Lynne Rienner, 2000), 113–36; Indra de Soysa, "Paradise Is a Bazaar? Greed, Creed, and Governance in Civil War, 1989–99," *Journal of Peace Research* 39, no. 4 (2002): 395–416; Michael L. Ross, "What Do We Know about Natural Resources and Civil War?" *Journal of Peace Research* 41, no. 3 (2004): 337–56; Michael L. Ross, "How Do Natural Resources Influence Civil War? Evidence from Thirteen Cases," *International Organization* 58, no. 1 (2004): 35–67.

12. Michael L. Ross, "The Political Economy of the Resource Curse," *World Politics* 51, no. 2 (1999): 320–21; Jeffrey D. Sachs and Andrew M. Warner, "The Big Push, Natural Resource Booms, and Growth," *Journal of Development Economics* 59 (1999): 43–76.

13. Richard M. Auty, *Patterns of Development: Resources, Policy and Economic Growth* (London: Edward Arnold, 1995); Terry Lynn Karl, *The Paradox of Plenty: Oil Booms and Petro-States* (University of California Press, 1997).

14. de Soysa, "Paradise Is a Bazaar?" 120–22; Michael Renner, *The Anatomy of Resource Wars,* Worldwatch Paper 162 (Washington: Worldwatch Institute, 2002), 14–18.

15. Jeffrey D. Sachs and Andrew M. Warner, *Natural Resource Abundance and Economic Growth,* Development Discussion Paper 517a (Cambridge, Mass.: Harvard Institute for International Development, 1995).

16. Renner, *Anatomy of Resource Wars,* 32–35, 45–47.

17. Fred Pearce, "Blood Diamonds and Oil," *New Scientist,* June 29, 2002, 40.

18. Renner, *Anatomy of Resource Wars,* 45–47; Michael Watts, "Petro-Violence: Community, Extraction, and Political Ecology of a Mythic Commodity," in *Violent Environments,* ed. Nancy Lee Peluso and Michael Watts (Cornell University Press, 2001), 189–212.

19. Renner, *Anatomy of Resource Wars,* 10; Mohamed Suliman, *Civil War in Sudan: The Impact of Ecological Degradation,* Occasional Paper 4, Environment and Conflicts Project (Berne and Zurich: Swiss Peace Foundation and Center for Security Studies and Conflict Research, 1992); Mohamed Suliman, "Civil War in the Sudan: From Ethnic to Ecological Conflict," *Ecologist* 23, no. 3 (1993): 104–9.

20. Philippe Le Billon, "The Political Ecology of War: Natural Resources and Armed Conflicts," *Political Geography* 20 (2001): 569–70.

21. Karl, *Paradox of Plenty,* 47–48.

22. Richard M. Auty, *Resource Abundance and Economic Development: Improving the Performance of Resource-Rich Countries,* Research for Action 44 (Helsinki: World Institute for Development Economics and Research, 1998), 1; Karl, *Paradox of Plenty,* 15, 48–49, 52, 56–57; Ross, "Political Economy of the Resource Curse," 311, 319–20.

23. Kahl, *States, Scarcity, and Civil Strife,* chap. 2.

24. Jack A. Goldstone and others, *State Failure Task Force Report: Phase III Findings* (McLean, Va.: Science Applications International Corporation, 2000), 14–16.

25. United Nations Population Division, *World Population Prospects: The 2004 Revision* (New York, 2005).

26. World Bank, *World Development Report 2003,* 4.

27. World Wildlife Fund, *Living Planet Report 2002,* 20.

5

Resource and Environmental Security

ANTHONY NYONG

AJOR CONTEMPORARY ECONOMIC and social issues are intimately linked with the quest for global poverty reduction, particularly poverty in developing countries. Today, people around the world, particularly in the developing world, are struggling to survive in the face of a multitude of environmental problems—the overuse of natural resources, the degradation of the ecosystem, and extreme climatic events such as floods, droughts, and hurricanes. These problems play an important role in increasing human vulnerability, undermining livelihoods and human well-being, threatening environmental security, and potentially generating or exacerbating conflict.[1] The past two decades have witnessed the intensification of the debate concerning the role that the environment plays in creating and exacerbating environmental insecurity and the impact that this has on poverty, particularly in the developing nations whose economies are largely dependent on the ecosystem.

Although environmental factors play an important role in creating environmental insecurity, other factors also are known to play significant roles. Such factors include poverty, income inequality, rapid population growth, poor governance, globalization, and a high disease burden. These factors interact with environmental problems to put enormous pressure on the social fabric of many communities and consequently precipitating insecurity that often leads to conflicts. Recent research attention on environmental security has largely focused on environmental resource-driven violent conflicts. The concept of environmental security should go beyond violent conflicts and the struggle for scarce environmental resources. In the coming

decades, accelerating environmental insecurity resulting from resource competition will aggravate global poverty and hamper the achievement of sustainable development, particularly of the Millennium Development Goals
(MDGs) in developing countries. Environmental security should therefore
expand in scope to include issues that could reduce society's vulnerability to
all forms of environmental threats, particularly poverty.

Poverty is both a cause and result of environmental insecurity. One way in
which poverty is entrenched in the society is through the uneven distribution
of and access to resources. Geographically, the poorest segments of the population live in the most degraded and marginal lands and economically do not
have access to most environmental goods and services. For instance, about 40
percent of Africa's population lives on marginal lands characterized as arid or
semiarid.[2] Though about 70 percent of the least developed countries are in
Africa, about 40 percent of them lie wholly or partially in these arid and
semiarid lands. In sub-Saharan Africa, for instance, poverty is a major factor
in environmental degradation. Poor people often adopt practices that
degrade the environment because survival, rather than long-term sustainability, is their ultimate goal. At the same time, when conflicts do occur, it is the
poor with the least resources to draw upon who are affected the most; a
majority of them are forced to flee their homes and end up as environmental
refugees. Poverty is therefore a potent and very destructive force in our present generation, and if it is not eradicated, world peace will be constantly
threatened. This chapter argues that reducing poverty requires an enhance-
ment of environmental security and that this largely is dependent on equitable access to and use of resources—ecological and nonecological.

The chapter is organized as follows. The next section presents a theoretical
basis for understanding the concepts of resources and environmental security,
which have become very controversial among scholars. It also provides the link
between resources and environmental security. It argues that both resource
scarcity and resource abundance—acting through other socioeconomic filters
such as poor governance, poverty, and rapid population growth—can threaten
environmental security. The section also discusses the threats from climate
variability and change, particularly in Africa. These threats have become major
global issues, and their potential ravages are so severe that they could nullify
efforts to secure meaningful and sustainable development, particularly in
developing countries. In the third section, two case studies are presented to
illustrate the role resources play in environmental insecurity and conflicts. This
is followed by a discussion of the implications of these insecurities for poverty
reduction, particularly in developing countries. The next section presents

guidelines for managing environmental conflicts, and the chapter ends with a set of recommendations and a conclusion.

Conceptual Issues

In this section, the concepts of resources and environmental security are presented and a definition is attempted for both terms within the context of this chapter. This is important because both terms mean different things to different people given that there are no universally accepted definitions for them. The section also presents a theoretical framework for understanding the relationship between resources and environmental security.

Resources

Resources comprise those basic material and social, tangible and intangible assets that human societies require for survival and growth. These assets can be classified as natural, economic/financial, physical, and social.[3] In the context of environmental security, many scholars normally view resources only from the narrow perspectives of environmental resources or natural assets, such as natural resource stocks (soil, water, air, genetic resources, and so on) and environmental services (hydrological cycle, pollution sinks, for example). This chapter takes a broader view of resources, for it is not only environmental resources that could precipitate environmental insecurity but also nonecological resources. The presence or absence of these nonecological resources can directly create insecurity or can interact with environmental resources to bring about environmental insecurity. Also, the ability to reduce or manage environmental insecurity depends on the availability of and access to these nonecological resources.

Environmental Security

Although there is no standard and universally accepted definition of environmental security, in this chapter "environmental security" refers to the protection of humans and societies from environmental, social, and cultural threats that undermine human security and the sustainable development of societies. The UN *Human Development Report 1994* identified seven interrelated dimensions of human security: economic, food, health, environmental, personal, community, and political.[4] It is therefore important that environmental security be seen as an integral part of human security.

Most studies of environmental security focus largely on conflicts, and indeed violent conflicts. "Conflicts" generally refer to the range of arguments, tensions, and violent altercations that occur both within and between concerned groups.[5] Conflicts are normal to everyday life and in themselves are not bad. It is the means that are often taken to resolve conflicts that are a threat to environmental security. Because environmental insecurity may not necessarily end in conflicts, focusing only on conflicts may mask potential threats and vulnerabilities that could threaten the existence of human populations and societies. Environmental security therefore should go beyond conflicts and conflict resolution to include the adverse effects on important human and societal functions and structures. Among these are factors that affect societal and social integrity, identity, and sovereignty, with the bottom line being about societal survival and peaceful existence.

Following from this is the notion that environmental security should be pursued at both spatial and temporal scales. At the spatial scale, it should transcend global, international, national, community, household, and individual levels; whereas at the temporal scale, it should include an intergenerational dimension because actions taken today will have implications for the security of future generations. Environmental security is not a snapshot in time, something that can be achieved and forgotten about. It should be sustained and sustainable; hence, the consideration of environmental security should not be just for the present but also for future generations.

Although environmental security is at the root of sustainable development, the two terms are not synonymous; in practice, however, the concerns of both concepts may often intersect. Environmental security is an essential component to achieve sustainable development. Because development and sustainability are conflictual, perfect environmental security is hardly obtainable or definable. Yet environmental security should at the least aim to minimize environmental damage and risk through the proper management of resources, reduction in the adverse effects of environmental changes and risks, and the avoidance or prompt resolution of environment-related tensions and conflicts. Environmental security is not an abstract phenomenon that cannot be quantified; rather, it can be identified, measured, and monitored using indicators such as access to good-quality water and sanitation, sufficient consumption patterns, human and societal vulnerability in the face of environmental changes, and changes in the environment related to morbidity, life expectancy, and the like.

Links between Resources and Environmental Security

The relationship between environment and security has been the focus of research among two communities in the past three decades: environmental scientists looking at the security implications of environmental change; and the security community, looking at new definitions of national security that embrace environmental threats. A common thread that runs through these two communities is the fact that environmental security is basically an issue of environmentally induced human conflicts exacerbated by the increasingly widening gap between the supply of and demand for environmental resources.

The recent entry of social scientists into the debate has added two new dimensions to the debate. First, it has challenged the direct link between the environment and conflict. It is difficult to point to a single factor as being responsible for the emergence, escalation, or protraction of conflict.[6] Second, it has highlighted the role played by other intervening nonecological factors. For instance, the intervening role played by such factors as population growth, demographic structure, and population distribution has been noted.[7]

Potential threats in the relationship between humans and environmental resources, and related conflicts among humans, underlie the notion of environmental insecurity. Two schools of thought with various explanations have emerged regarding the underlying causes of these threats.[8] One school of thought adopts a neo-Malthusian model and lays the blame on resource scarcity.[9] Three types of resource scarcity can be readily identified: economic scarcity, which refers to the quantity of a resource; ecological scarcity, which refers to its quality; and structural scarcity, which is caused by an unbalanced distribution of resources that severely affects less powerful groups in society.

Resource scarcity can lead to declining agricultural production, which is the mainstay of most economies of developing countries; to economic hardship; to migrations of people from areas of environmental stress; and to tensions within and among groups.[10] When resource scarcity reduces the ability of a state to meet the needs of its population, it increases the vulnerability of citizens. Such vulnerabilities are manifested in poor access to vital resources such as health, food, water and sanitation, and education. This creates dissatisfaction that can lead to declining state authority, which sooner or later nurtures violent collective action.

The second school of thought works on the "greed theory," where powerful groups appropriate most of the resources to themselves, excluding what is often the less powerful majority of the population. This ultimately creates negative economic and political effects, such as slow growth, poor governance, weak institutions, and political instability. Both models of conflicts are plausible, and this chapter attempts to integrate both as drivers of environmental insecurity. Whether the explanation is scarcity or greed, struggles over resources are at the center of most environmental insecurities and conflicts. However, the causal process of environmental insecurity is complex, and environmental factors are only one dimension of the problem.

Although attempts have been made to understand environmental conflicts, their link with global poverty has been less understood and investigated. The connection between the environment and the security of local communities through the mechanism of livelihoods is emerging as the "missing link" between resources, environmental security, and poverty. The sudden and rapid loss of livelihoods and the impoverishment stemming from unbalanced access to critical resources deepen the fault lines prevalent in almost all societies and mobilize angry and underemployed people to rise up in arms.

Climate Change and Environmental Security

Climate change is fast gaining notoriety as the greatest threat to environmental security in this century. The Third Assessment Report of the Intergovernmental Panel on Climate Change has noted that human activities have significantly contributed to global warming.[11] Observational records show that during the twentieth century, the world's average temperatures increased by approximately 0.6 °C, with the five warmest years occurring between 1998 and 2005.[12] Much higher temperatures have been observed on continental landmasses, as in Africa. This global warming has brought with it observed undesirable consequences, such as increases in extreme events, including floods and droughts.[13] The index of seasonal destructiveness of hurricanes has increased since 1975 at the global level.[14] No part of the world has been spared these disastrous consequences. The heat wave that occurred in Europe in 2003 claimed several thousand lives and put a serious strain on the medical infrastructure in several European countries.[15] Climate change has been modeled to have caused the loss of 150,000 lives since the 1970s, particularly in Africa.[16]

However, it is generally noted that poor and developing countries are most vulnerable to the effects of climate change, with Africa being the hardest hit because a greater proportion of its economy depends on the ecosystem. This is in addition to the fact that it has the least resources required to cope with the impact of climate change. For instance, in Africa, observed damage from the 1999–2000 flood disaster in Mozambique was estimated at more than $427 million.[17] Other observed changes include the almost complete disappearance of Lake Chad and the near-complete melting of the glacier on Mount Kilimanjaro. These have had disastrous consequences for the livelihoods of large populations that depend on these ecosystem resources. Climate-related diseases such as malaria are reemerging, even in previously controlled areas. The economic burden of malaria is estimated at an average annual reduction in economic growth of 1.3 percent for those African countries with the highest burden, with $12 billion lost to the African continent's gross domestic product annually.[18]

Climate models predict that mean surface temperatures could increase by between 1.5 °C and 6 °C by 2100, though with projections of up to 9 °C in some parts of Africa.[19] This will be accompanied by a rise in the sea level of almost a meter by the end of the century. Accompanying threats from such temperature and sea-level rises include a decline in food productivity, with additional millions of people, particularly in Africa, at risk of hunger; the possibility that several large coastal cities could be inundated; and severe negative effects on the economies of several countries that are dependent on tourism and agriculture.[20]

Climate change has created new environmental conflict hot spots that could lead to a significant increase in national and international conflicts over shared environmental resources, such as water and land. Climate change is a pressing poverty issue. It can nullify efforts to secure meaningful and sustainable development in poor communities and countries.[21] Climate change could ruin whatever modest gains that poor countries, particularly in Africa, have achieved in the past decades. No other single issue presents such a clear and present danger to the future welfare of the world's poor.[22]

Case Studies of Environmental Insecurity Hot Spots

This section reviews two case studies of resource-related environmental insecurities and eventual conflicts. Although both studies illustrate armed conflicts and what have turned out to be major international and humanitarian disasters, the goal here is to bring out the role that resources have played in threatening environmental security and precipitating such disasters. Both studies illustrate a typical relationship between humans and resources and typify resource greed exacerbated by resource scarcity.

The first case study, on the environmental insecurity that led to the well-known Rwandan genocide, is a result of what Homer-Dixon refers to as "resource capture."[23] This is a situation in which a fall in the quantity and quality of renewable resources combines with population growth to encourage powerful or advantaged groups within a society to shift resources in their favor, usually producing acute environmental scarcity for poorer and weaker groups whose claims to resources are opposed by the much stronger groups, leading to conflicts. The second case study, on the Darfur crisis in Sudan, illustrates the principle of "ecological marginalization."

Land Resources and Violent Conflict: The Rwanda Genocide

Although the general opinion regarding the Rwandan conflict tends to place the cause at the doorstep of ethnic political rivalry, the genocide was in reality the product of complex interactions among demographic pressure, land degradation, inequitable access to and shortage of land resources, unequal education opportunities, the unemployment of rural youth, and unequal representation in power.[24] Rapid population growth and deepening poverty were becoming major threats to environmental security in Rwanda. The population had increased more than threefold over a period of fifty years, from 1.9 million in 1948 to 7.5 million in 1992. Coffee, the state's major foreign exchange earner, witnessed a sharp fall on the world market, with the value of exports dropping from $60 per capita per year in the period 1976–79 to $13 in 1991. The wealth divide was increasing, with the rich getting richer and the poor becoming poorer across all ethnic groups.

Frequent droughts, interacting with population pressure and deepening poverty, were accelerating soil degradation, leading to further declines in land productivity. This process drove rural inhabitants into a vicious cycle of poverty, hopelessness, and helplessness, which was ultimately responsible for the famine of the mid-1980s (box 5-1) that caused hundreds of deaths of humans and livestock.[25] The famine—in addition to the uncontrolled resource capture, including political resources, by powerful elites—led to a general dissatisfaction among the poor with the state for its inability to provide for their needs and welfare.

The government's failure to acknowledge and address such grievances prompted political dissension and presented opposition leaders with an opportunity to wage war against the government. The war basically was motivated by a struggle for political power and state resources among the elites. However, when the violence eventually erupted, it started in areas with heightened vulnerability, where poverty had become endemic and where people whose very existence was threatened took up arms to fight the rich, whom they accused of capturing all the resources meant for the state.

When the country became deeply entangled in the war, the political class was able to recenter the dialectic from rich versus poor to Tutsi against Hutu.[26] The conflicts that ensued potentially created opportunities to address the issues of environmental insecurity that were at the root of the conflict.

BOX 5-1
Famine and Inequitable Access to Resources in Rwanda

In the 1980s, the inequality in access to land resources in Rwanda caused severe structural scarcity for the rural population, the majority of whom were affected by ecological marginalization. By 1984, about 43 percent of poorer families owned only 15 percent of cultivated lands, with average land holding size varying from less than 0.25 to 0.75 hectares. About 50 percent of rural families had to hire land to produce for their basic subsistence needs. On the other end of the spectrum, 16 percent of land-rich families owned 43 percent of cultivated lands, with an average land holding size of more than 1 hectare. As a result, poor farmers were squeezed in steep unproductive lands, where the soil is constantly removed by erosion, becoming in-situ ecological refugees. By 1989, about 50 percent of cultivated soils had slopes higher than 18 percent. As a result of this imbalance, about two-thirds of the population of Rwanda was unable to meet the minimum food energy requirements of 2,100 calories per person per day. As the hungry were not only landless or near-landless, but also earned little or no monetary revenue, there was a structural famine in 1988–89 whose roots were embedded in the inequitable and disorderly land tenure. (Source: James K. Gasana, "Natural Resource Scarcity and Violence in Rwanda," in *Conserving the Peace: Resources, Livelihoods and Security* [London: International Union for the Conservation of Nature, 2002].)

Unfortunately, efforts to resolve the conflict placed undue emphasis on the ethnic dimensions of the conflict and on the use of arms. The use of arms to resolve conflicts is a threat to peace and security. There were no attempts to tackle the root causes of the conflict, such as the unequal distribution of land and the deepening poverty caused by declining agricultural productivity.

Darfur: Ethnic Cleansing or Environmental Conflict?

Sudan, which was devastated by civil war between the north and south from 1966 to 1972, is again in the news because of the violence that has risen to national and international dimensions in the Darfur region. Though ethnic cleansing has been given as the reason for this conflict, it is an environmental conflict over access to land resources, compounded by other social factors such as high population growth, poverty, and a lack of government presence in the form of development.

The Darfur region has historically been faced with harsh environmental conditions. Annual rainfall varies from almost nothing in the arid north to about 800 millimeters in the southern part, with the Jabal Marrah highlands receiving about 1,000 millimeters, and mean averages between 75 and 200 millimeters.[27] Sudan has experienced a precipitation decrease of nearly 50 percent over the past fifteen years. Consequently, the periodic droughts suffered by certain regions of Sudan, including Darfur, have increased in frequency and intensity. Five major droughts have been recorded in Sudan. The first was in 1896, and the second occurred between 1910 and 1920. The third was between 1940 and 1945, while the fourth occurred between 1970 and 1973 during the notorious Sahelian drought episode. The fifth occurred in 1984. These droughts ultimately led to severe water scarcities and land degradation in the region.

These long periods of drought, which have particularly affected the northern parts of Sudan for the past four decades, resulting in mounting poverty and widespread population movement, have provided the causes for conflict. During the terrible droughts of the 1980s, nomads of mostly Arab origin, living mainly in northern Sudan, were faced with dried-out natural pastures and herded their livestock onto the land of the sedentary farmers of the southern tribes, such as the Fur. The nomads allowed their herds to graze the farmers' crops, and the farmers, suffering just as much from the drought, defended their land and crops, resulting in several conflicts.

With state power largely residing in the north among the Jellaba (Sudanese of Arab origin) and with the marginalization of the south (table 5-1), the Jellaba had begun a number of schemes based on the oil, water, and abundant land resources in the south by the 1970s. The southern Sudanese became increasingly wary of the development projects that the ruling Sudanese of Arab origin were implementing in the south.

These projects were perceived as intending to bring benefits only to the Jellaba. The southern Sudanese and the ecologically marginalized northern Sudanese, fearing they might not have access to the wealth that would be created by the exploitation of the rich resources from the south, incited grassroots mobilization against these projects. These marginalized people believed that to be able to negotiate with the Arab-controlled government of Sudan, they would have to take up arms and be a real threat to the government. With the formation of the Sudan People's Liberation Army and the Sudan

Table 5-1. Comparison between Attributes of Northern and Southern Sudan

Attribute	Northern Sudan	Southern Sudan
Ethnic/cultural diversity	Low	High
Natural resource base	Low	High
Infrastructure investment	High	Low
International linkages and trade	High	Low
Economic livelihoods	Commercial agriculture, trade	Subsistence agriculture, pastoralism

Source: J. Switzer, *Oil and Violence in Sudan* (Nairobi: IUCN–World Conservation Union Commission on Environmental, Economic, and Social Policy, 2002).

People's Liberation Movement, these people now had a means to pursue action to address their alleged marginalization and insecurity.[28]

The current conflict in Darfur resulted when a civil war between the government of Sudan and the two rebel movements erupted on a complex ethnic line. The government resorted to force to crush the rebels' movements, but the army was struggling to fight the well-trained, well-armed, and well-motivated rebels. The government allegedly opted for an alliance with the Arab pastoralist militias, which have a vested interest in fighting this war, because most of the rebels were from competing tribes. All the peace accords and efforts to resolve this conflict have failed to address its underlying causes.

Although people have come to see the Darfur conflict as a case of ethnic cleansing, it should be borne in mind that ecological imbalances, a scarcity of water, deforestation, the mismanagement of natural resources, an alleged inequality in the distribution of available resources and national projects, and a lack of cooperation have all been main factors in the conflict.

Implications for Poverty Reduction

The widening poverty gap between developed and developing countries led to the adoption of the Millennium Declaration in September 2000 by the UN General Assembly. The Millennium Development Goals form an ambitious global agenda to eradicate extreme poverty and hunger. The targets set for 2015 are to halve the proportion of people living in extreme poverty and hunger. The Millennium Declaration, however, moved away from seeing poverty only in monetary and economic terms and toward incorporating other aspects of human security, such as education, health, environment, water, and human rights. In doing so, it provided the opportunity to address the broad social and political questions that are central to human security.

Although several countries are striving to achieve these noble goals, environmental conflicts are not only making it impossible for several others, particularly in Africa, to even position themselves on the right path but could even undo whatever small achievements there may have been. Environmental insecurity, violent conflicts, and poverty are self-reinforcing. As the two case studies examined here have shown, particularly the Rwanda case, the poor are more likely to resort to violence than the rich and secure. Violence further exacerbates poverty; besides disrupting economic activities, vital financial resources that could have been used for developmental purposes are diverted to prosecuting armed conflicts. Resources diverted by conflict away from development are estimated at $1 billion a year in Central Africa and more than $800 million in West Africa.[29]

There is a loss of investors' confidence in conflict-prone economies. As a result, there is a likely strong negative correlation between conflicts and foreign direct investment. Development assistance also suffers when major donor countries are involved in armed conflicts because enormous resources are channeled toward fighting them. The decline in such funds could have severe negative effects, particularly in countries that largely depend on foreign aid.

One major asset in creating wealth or reducing vulnerability to human insecurity is human capital, the strength of the productive labor force. Armed conflicts have caused the death of several millions of people in Africa. Women and children are often the most vulnerable and worst-affected social category. Women traditionally are responsible for about 70 percent of agricultural production in Africa. Their vulnerability, in turn, affects agricultural productivity on the continent. Their traditional productive and reproductive roles in the household have also been challenged as thousands of them have been raped and turned into sexual slaves, disrupting family values and societal norms. Also, sub-Saharan Africa has the highest rate of HIV/AIDS in the world, with conflict zones having the worst incidence. A big part of the blame for Africa's HIV/AIDS pandemic falls on wars, soldiers, and the culture of militarization. In Liberia, for instance, the HIV/AIDS incidence rate rose from 1 percent in the prewar period to 16 percent in 2002.[30]

Environmental conflicts breed environmental refugees. These refugees are largely destitute and do not contribute optimally to development in their settled regions. They become a burden on the state and the neighboring regions. Their emotional and psychological traumas are often not taken into account even though these reduce people's dignity and erode their ability to achieve optimal levels of human security. Food security is a particular challenge for environmental refugees. They often cannot grow food in refugee camps; hence the many "starving villages" that dot the continent.

Conflicts most certainly lead to famines and malnutrition. In the Horn of Africa, armed conflicts in the 1980s and 1990s resulted in a decline in life expectancy of ten to twenty years, per capita income decreased by 50 percent, famine became endemic, and other indicators of human security such as health and education also worsened. And the conflict and crisis in Darfur has resulted in high rates of global acute malnutrition and severe acute malnutrition among children under five years of age. In cases of environmental conflict, children suffer the most and are the most vulnerable to morbidity and mortality. Child mortality rates in Africa are by far the worst in the world; a total of 4 million African children under the age of five die each year. Malnutrition, for example, is a contributing factor in at least half of all child deaths, because malnourished children cannot resist common infections as readily as adequately nourished children and, when infected, have a much higher risk of complications and death.[31]

Other ways in which environmental conflicts could constrain poverty reduction are in the destruction of infrastructure and developmental installations. In Africa, for instance, the low level of transportation facilities is cited as one of the main factors in underdevelopment.[32] During environmental conflicts, infrastructure is destroyed, further leading to underdevelopment, such as is occurring in southern Sudan and in the Niger Delta region of Nigeria.

Conclusion and Recommendations

Environmental security has become a critical issue in contemporary development, reflecting a common concern for the implications of environmental change on sustainable development. The term has generated considerable confusion and contentious debate on how the environment and security are linked. Attention should shift from the narrow focus on conflicts that must be resolved using a statist approach to a more interdisciplinary and integrative approach that sees environmental security as a crucial component of the broader concept of "human security." Through this integrative approach, the individual and, by extension, the local and global community are identified as the object of security.

Moreover, the research agenda on environmental security should move beyond basic arguments about whether conflict is an outcome of resource scarcity—itself often determined by sociopolitical power relations—to preventing such scarcity through proper management by strengthening institutions and the processes of governance and making them more responsive and effective. Attention should focus more on the inequitable distribution of resources and the power that comes with it than on violent conflict as the principal source of insecurity. As demonstrated in the case studies, structural inequalities—particularly land distribution and access to political resources—are major factors in environmental conflicts in Africa. Though resources play a major role in environmental conflicts, they are only one dimension of the problem. It is important that we understand the interplay among political, economic, and social factors and how they interact with the environment to cause environmental insecurity and precipitate violent conflicts. Environmental security may be unattainable in any absolute sense, but continuous attempts must be made to prevent, manage, and resolve environmental conflicts, particularly armed conflicts, because of their potential role in aggravating global poverty.

Although this chapter does not boast solutions for preventing, managing, and resolving environmental conflicts, such solutions would require approaches that are diverse, multidimensional, and located at many levels, from local to international. A few guiding principles can be suggested.

First, conflict, as has been illustrated, is one symptom of environmental insecurity. It is not the cause and neither is it the final outcome of environmental insecurity. The first step in resolving any issue of environmental insecurity is to assess the root causes of such insecurities. Structural inequality in access to resources is usually at the center of most environmental insecurities. Efforts should be made to improve equity in access to resources at the local, national, and global levels, particularly where the environment is seen as a public good. The best way to manage conflicts is to prevent the conflict from occurring in the first place.

Second, where environmental conflicts occur, their management should first of all explore peaceful conflict resolution approaches. Research should be carried out to identify key intervention points at which policymakers might be able to alter the causal processes linking human activity, environmental degradation, and conflict. Most resource-related environmental conflicts start at a local scale and grow in magnitude. It is important that such conflicts be first addressed at the local level as they occur. Traditional institutions have well-entrenched mechanisms for dealing with such conflicts. Where such mechanisms exist, they should be explored and used. When such conflicts assume a national or international dimension, the United Nations or appropriate regional institutions should be tasked with the responsibility of managing and resolving them. Several mechanisms are in place to handle violent conflicts in Africa. Most of them adopt state-centered approaches that attempt political and military solutions. There is a need to situate conflicts within the environmental security and development nexus and to redefine development in a way that goes beyond state-centeredness to include, among other things, increased participation by civil society groups in the development process.

Third, efforts should be made to develop early warning signals for environmental conflicts. These could involve the identification of major environmental problems and principal social effects and the possible threats to human security.

Fourth and very important, to break the cycle of environmental conflicts in Africa, efforts must be made to transform the socioeconomic and political conditions that promote poverty on the continent. This transformation can only take place where there is good governance and democratization. African governments are increasingly realizing that such transformations can only happen from within the continent. This realization informed the establishment of the New Economic Partnership for African Development and the African Union to address Africa's development needs, of which human security is a crucial part.

Notes

1. Michael Renner and Hilary French, "Linkages between Environment, Population and Development: Environmental Change and Security," in *Project Report,* issue 10 (Washington: Woodrow Wilson International Center for Scholars, 2004).

2. United Nations Environment Program, *Africa Environment Outlook: Past, Present and Future Perspectives* (Nairobi, 2002).

3. Ian Scoones, *Sustainable Rural Livelihoods: A Framework for Analysis,* Working Paper 72 (Brighton: Institute of Development Studies, University of Sussex, 1998).

4. United Nations Development Program, *Human Development Report 1994* (New York, 1994).

5. Bakut Tswah Bakut, "The Environment, Peace and Conflict in Africa," in *Introduction to Peace and Conflict Studies in West Africa,* ed. Shedrack G. Best (Lagos: Spectrum Books, 2005).

6. Stephen Ademola Faleti, "Theories of Social Conflict," in *Introduction to Peace and Conflict Studies in West Africa,* ed. Best.

7. Paul Ehrlich and Anne Ehrlich, *The Population Explosion* (London: Hutchinson, 1990).

8. Nils Petter Gleditsch, "Beyond Scarcity vs. Abundance: A Policy Research Agenda for Natural Resources and Conflict," in *Understanding Environment, Conflict and Cooperation* (New York: United Nations Environment Program, 2004).

9. Thomas F. Homer-Dixon, "On the Threshold: Environmental Changes as Causes of Acute Conflict," *International Security* 16, no. 2 (1991).

10. Thomas F. Homer-Dixon, "Environmental Scarcities and Violent Conflict: Evidence from Cases," *International Security* 19, no. 1 (1994).

11. Intergovernmental Panel on Climate Change, *Impacts, Adaptation, and Vulnerability: Contribution of Working Group II to the IPCC Third Assessment Report*, ed. James J. McCarthy, Osvaldo F. Canziani, Neil A. Leary, David J. Dokken, and Kasey S. White (Cambridge University Press, 2001).

12. United Nations Environment Program, *Africa Environment Outlook: Past, Present and Future Perspectives*.

13. Intergovernmental Panel on Climate Change, *Impacts, Adaptation, and Vulnerability;* Z. W. Kundzewicz, "Is the Frequency and Intensity of Flooding Changing in Europe?" in *Extreme Weather Events and Public Health Responses*, ed. Wilhem Kirch, Bettina Menne, and Roberto Bertollini (Berlin: Springer, 2005).

14. Kerry Emmanuel, "Increasing Destructiveness of Tropical Cyclones over the Past 30 Years," *Nature* 436 (2005).

15. Stéphanie Vandentorren and Pascal Empereur-Bissonnet, "Health Impact of the 2003 Heat Wave in France," in *Extreme Weather Events and Public Health Responses*, ed. Kirch, Menne, and Bertollini.

16. Anthony J. McMichael and others, "Global Climate Change," in *Comparative Quantification of Health Risks: Global and Regional Burden of Disease due to Selected Major Risk Factors*, vol. 2, ed. Majid Ezzaoti and others (Geneva: World Health Organization, 2004).

17. R. Hirji, P. Johnson, P. Maro, and T. Matiza-Chiuta, eds., *Defining and Mainstreaming Environmental Sustainability in Water Resources Management in Southern Africa* (Maseru, Harare, and Washington: SADC, IUCN, SARDC, and World Bank, 2002).

18. Jeffrey Sachs and Pia Malaney, "The Economic and Social Burden of Malaria," *Nature* 416 (2002): 581.

19. Intergovernmental Panel on Climate Change, *Impacts, Adaptation, and Vulnerability;* Anthony Okon Nyong and Isabelle Niang-Diop, "Impacts of Climate Change in the Tropics: The African Experience," in *Avoiding Dangerous Climate Change*, ed. H. J. Schellnhuber and others (Cambridge University Press, 2006).

20. M. Parry, C. Rosenzweig, A. Iglesias, M. Livermore, and G. Fisher, "Effects of Climate Change on Global Food Production under SRES Emissions and Socioeconomic Scenarios," *Global Environmental Change* 14, no. 1 (2004): 53–67; P. G. Jones and P. K. Thornton, "The Potential Impacts of Climate Change on Maize Production in Africa and Latin America in 2055," *Global Environmental Change* 13 (2003): 51–59.

21. African Development Bank and others, *Poverty and Climate Change: Reducing the Vulnerability of the Poor through Adaptation Part 1* (Dakar: African Development Bank, 2003). This report was prepared by these organizations: African Development Bank; Asian Development Bank; Department for International Development, United Kingdom; Directorate General for Development, European Commission; Federal Ministry for Economic Cooperation and Development, Germany; Ministry of Foreign Affairs–Development Cooperation; Netherlands Organization for Economic Cooperation and Development; United Nations Development Program; United Nations Environment Program; and World Bank.

22. Christian Aid, *The Climate of Poverty: Facts, Fears and Hope* (London, 2006); A. Simms, J. Magrath, and H. Reid, *Africa: Up in Smoke?* (London: International Institute for Environment and Development, 2004).

23. Homer-Dixon, "Environmental Scarcities and Violent Conflict," 9.

24. James K. Gasana, "Factors of Ethnic Conflict in Rwanda and Instruments for a Durable Peace," in *Federalism against Ethnicity: Institutional, Legal and Democratic Instruments to Prevent Violent Minority Conflicts,* ed. G. Bächler (Zurich: Verlag Rüeger Chur, 1997).

25. James K. Gasana, "Natural Resource Scarcity and Violence in Rwanda," in *Conserving the Peace: Resources, Livelihoods and Security* (London: International Union for the Conservation of Nature, 2002).

26. Ibid.

27. Abdalla Ahmed Abdalla, "Environmental Degradation and Conflict in Darfur: Experiences and Development Options," in *Environmental Degradation as a Cause for Conflict in Darfur: Conference Proceedings* (Geneva: University for Peace, 2006), 87–94.

28. Daniel Schwartz and Ashbindu Singh, *Environmental Conditions, Resources, and Conflicts: An Introductory Overview and Data Collection* (New York: United Nations Environment Program, 1999).

29. Victor Adebola Adetula, "Development, Conflict and Peace-Building in Africa," in *Introduction to Peace and Conflict Studies in West Africa,* ed. Best.

30. Ibid.

31. Robert E. Black, Saul S. Morris, and Jennifer Bryce, "Where and Why Are 10 Million Children Dying Every Year?" *Lancet,* 361 (2003): 2226–34.

32. Jeffrey Sachs and others, "Ending Africa's Poverty Trap," *Bookings Papers on Economic Activity* 1 (2004): 117–240.

6

The Demographics of Political Violence: Youth Bulges, Insecurity, and Conflict

HENRIK URDAL

YOUTH OFTEN PLAY a prominent role in political violence, and the existence of a "youth bulge" has historically been associated with times of political crisis.[1] Generally, it has been observed that young males are the main protagonists of criminal as well as political violence.

The question is whether countries with youthful age structures, or "youth bulges,"[2] are more likely to experience internal armed conflict, terrorism, and riots. The issue has received increasing attention during the past decade following the more general debate over security implications of population pressure and resource scarcity. In "The Coming Anarchy," Robert Kaplan argues that anarchy and the crumbling of nation-states will be attributed to demographic and environmental factors in the future.[3] More recently, youth bulges have become a popular explanation for current political instability in the Arab world and for recruitment to international terrorist networks. In a background article surveying the root causes of the September 11, 2001, terrorist attacks on the United States, *Newsweek* editor Fareed Zakaria argues that youth bulges combined with slow economic and social change have provided a foundation for an Islamic resurgence in the Arab world.[4] Samuel Huntington claims that youth bulges are the major reason for higher political violence levels in Muslim countries (box 6-1).

This chapter draws on two prominent theoretical perspectives concerning opportunity versus motive for civil war, as well as on recent advances in economic demography, to identify a possible causal explanation for why cohort size in itself and under particular conditions may cause political violence. The

BOX 6-1
A Clash of Generations?

"I don't think Islam is any more violent than any other religions. . . . But the key factor is the demographic factor. Generally speaking, the people who go out and kill other people are males between the ages of 16 and 30. During the 1960s, 1970s, and 1980s, there were high birthrates in the Muslim world, and this has given rise to a huge youth bulge. But the bulge will fade. Muslim birthrates are going down; in fact, they have dropped dramatically in some countries." —Samuel P. Huntington, "So, Are Civilizations at War?" *The Observer,* October 21, 2001.

empirical results point to a clear statistical relationship between youth bulges and an increased risk of both internal armed conflict, terrorism, and riots.[5]

Youth Bulges and Political Violence: Greed and Grievance

The literature on youth bulges has focused in particular on spontaneous and low-intensity unrest, such as nonviolent protests, riots, and rebellions. It is argued here, however, that youth bulges may also increase the risk of more organized forms of political violence, such as internal armed conflict. The chapter draws on two of the dominant and competing theoretical traditions in the study of civil war, one focusing on opportunity and the other on the motive for conflict.

Both the opportunity and the motive perspectives are macro-level frameworks that attempt to explain events essentially consisting of a series of individual decisions—whether to join a rebel or terrorist organization or not—by focusing on economic, political, and social structural features. The opportunity literature, often termed the *greed perspective,* has its roots in economic theory and focuses on the structural conditions that provide opportunities for a rebel group to wage war against a government.[6] These are conditions that provide a rebel group with the financial means to fight, or factors that reduce the cost of rebellion, such as unusually low recruitment costs for rebel soldiers. Former World Bank economist Paul Collier has suggested that relatively large youth cohorts may be a factor that reduces recruitment costs through the abundant supply of rebel labor with low opportunity cost, increasing the risk of armed conflict.[7] According to the opportunity perspective, rebellion is feasible only when the potential gain from joining is so high and the expected costs so low that rebel recruits will favor joining over alternative income-earning opportunities.

Although opportunity may be the most important determinant of civil war, this does not necessarily mean that actors cannot also have strong motives.[8] The motive-oriented tradition, or *grievance perspective,* has its origins in relative deprivation theory and tends to see the eruption of political violence as a rational means to redress economic or political grievances.[9] Motives for committing political violence can be economic—such as poverty, economic recession, or inequality—or political—such as a lack of democracy, the absence of minority representation, or the desire for self-governance. Most of the literature on youth bulges and political violence falls into this tradition. It focuses on how large youth cohorts facing institutional bottlenecks and unemployment, a lack of political openness, and crowding in urban centers may become aggrieved, paving the way for political violence.[10] But in its simplest form, the motive perspective overpredicts political violence; the existence of serious grievances is not sufficient for collective violent action to erupt.[11] The likelihood that motives will be redressed through political violence increases when opportunity arises from the availability of financial means, low costs, or a weak state.

The Mere Size of Youth Cohorts

The mere existence of an extraordinarily large pool of youth is a factor that lowers the cost of recruitment because the opportunity cost for a young person generally is low.[12] This is an assumption that hinges on the extent of alternative income-earning opportunities. If young people are left with no alternative but unemployment and poverty, they are increasingly likely to join a rebellion as an alternative way of generating an income. Higher levels of education among men may act to reduce the risk of political violence. Because educated men have better income-earning opportunities than uneducated ones, they would have more to lose and hence be less likely to join a rebellion.[13] A recent study based on interviews with young soldiers presents strong micro-level support for the expectation that poverty, a lack of schooling, and low alternative income opportunities are important reasons for joining a rebel group.[14]

New research in economic demography even suggests that the alternative costs of individuals belonging to larger youth cohorts are generally lower compared with members of smaller cohorts. According to the "cohort size" hypothesis, "other things being constant, the economic and social fortunes of a cohort (those born in a given year) tend to vary inversely with its relative size."[15] So not only do youth bulges provide an unusually high supply of individuals with low opportunity cost, but an individual belonging to a relatively large youth cohort generally also has a lower opportunity cost relative to a young person born into a smaller cohort.

The influence of the size of youth cohorts on unemployment is also emphasized in the motive-oriented literature on civil violence.[16] If the labor market cannot absorb a sudden surplus of young job seekers, a large pool of unemployed youths will generate strong frustration. In extreme cases, the challenge to employ large youth cohorts can appear overwhelming. In Saudi Arabia, approximately 4 million people will be added to the labor force during the next decade, equaling two-thirds of the current Saudi national workforce.[17] The socioeconomic problems associated with youth bulges may provide fertile ground for recruitment to terrorist organizations.[18]

The Demographic Dividend

Recent studies in economic demography suggest that the relationship between large youth cohorts and political violence may be muted if youth bulges precede significantly smaller cohorts. Economists and demographers have long discussed the allegedly negative impact of population growth rates on economic growth. Recently, this debate has been advanced by disaggregating the focus to look at the impact of growth among different age segments. Though high growth rates in the nonworking, or dependent, age groups are associated with lower economic growth, increases in the working-age population are positively associated with economic growth.[19] Thus, in areas where the demographic transition is well under way with sharply declining fertility rates, countries may experience a window of opportunity for economic development, often called a "demographic dividend," largely flowing from increased savings as the relative number of dependents decreases. Hence, the expectation is that youth bulges should be associated with less political violence in countries with declining fertility rates. This is consistent with the opportunity as well as the motive perspective. In countries with a lower dependency burden, the alternative cost of rebel labor will be higher. On the motive side of the coin, a reduction in the dependency burden implies greater employment and income prospects, reducing grievances.

Economic Growth

The overall economic performance of a society is an important factor determining the income forgone when a youth joins a rebel movement, and thus the opportunity for rebellion. Economic growth over a longer period may act as a proxy for new income opportunities.[20] For large youth cohorts, the economic climate at the time they enter into the labor market is particularly crucial. To the degree that income opportunities are determined by general economic performance, large youth cohorts are likely be rendered particularly susceptible to lower income opportunities when economic conditions generally deteriorate, reducing the income they forgo by signing up as rebels. The motive-oriented literature also shares the concern over economic decline. Youth belonging to large cohorts will be especially vulnerable to unemployment if their entry into the labor force coincides with periods of serious economic decline. Such coincidences may generate despair among young people that moves them toward the use of violence.[21]

Rapid Expansion in Higher Education

A tool that countries can exploit in order to respond to youth bulges is the expansion of higher education. Can this serve as a strategy to reduce the risk of political violence? As argued above, education is generally expected to increase the opportunity cost of rebel labor. This implies that rebel recruitment is more costly and rebellion less likely the higher the level of education in a society.[22] This is not inconsistent with the motive-oriented literature. However, it has been suggested that when countries respond to large youth cohorts by expanding opportunities for higher education, this may produce a much larger group of highly educated youths than can be accommodated in the normal economy. Unless the government is able and willing to absorb a surplus of university graduates into the public sector, as was done by the government of Egypt,[23] prevailing unemployment among highly educated youth segments may cause frustration and grievances that could motivate political violence. It has been argued that high unemployment among educated youth is one of the most destabilizing and potentially violent sociopolitical phenomena in any regime,[24] and that a rapid increase in the number of educated youths has preceded historical episodes of political upheaval.[25] It has been argued that the expansion of higher education in many countries in the Middle East, producing large classes of educated youth that the labor market cannot absorb, has had a radicalizing effect and provided new recruits to militant organizations in the area.[26]

A Lack of Democracy

When being used to assess the role of democracy, the opportunity and motive perspectives yield opposite predictions. The opportunity literature suggests that the opportunity for political violence is greater the less autocratic a state is, whereas the motive-oriented literature argues that the greater the political oppression and the lack of political rights, the greater the motive for political violence. Several empirical studies of regime type and civil conflict have found a curvilinear "inverted U" relationship between democracy and conflict, suggesting that starkly autocratic regimes and highly democratic societies are the most peaceful.[27] This relationship is assumed to arise as a result of both opportunity and motive, because semidemocratic regimes may have greater openings for conflict compared with autocratic states.

At the same time, a lack of political rights may also constitute a motive for conflict. It has been suggested by proponents of the motive perspective that when large youth groups aspiring to political positions are excluded from participation in the political process, they may engage in violent conflict behavior in an attempt to force democratic reform.[28] The potential for radical mobilization for terrorist organizations is argued to be greater when large educated youth cohorts are barred from social mobility by autocratic and patriarchal forms of governance.[29]

Urbanization

Although institutional crowding has been the major focus, geographic crowding has also been argued to generate motives for political violence.[30] Because terrorism is essentially an urban phenomenon, states undergoing rapid urbanization may be particularly likely to experience increased risks of terrorism.[31] If youth are abundant in a relatively small geographical area, this may increase the likelihood that grievances caused by crowding in the labor market or educational institutions will arise. Historically, the coincidence of youth bulges with rapid urbanization, especially in the context of unemployment and poverty, has been an important contributor to political violence.[32] Youth often constitute a disproportionately large part of rural-to-urban migrants; hence, in the face of large youth cohorts, strong urbanization may be expected to lead to an extraordinary crowding of youth in urban centers, potentially increasing the risk of political violence.

An Empirical Examination

The results of my internal armed conflict models suggest that the presence of youth bulges increases the risk of conflict outbreak significantly.[33] The statistical relationship holds even when controlling for a number of other factors—such as the level of development, democracy, and conflict history—and is also robust to a variety of technical specifications. *For each percentage point increase of youth in the adult population, the risk of conflict increases by more than 4 percent.* When youth make up more than 35 percent of the adult population, which they do in many developing countries, the risk of armed conflict is 150 percent higher than in countries with an age structure similar to most developed countries (see box 6-2).

A claim that youth bulges become particularly volatile when they pass a certain threshold does not seem to have any validity.[34] These bulges seem to be associated with a higher risk of conflict in countries with high dependency ratios, while countries that are well under way in their demographic transitions are likely to experience a "peace dividend."

If youth bulges increase the likelihood of armed conflict, how and why do they matter? Though the risk of conflict does not seem to increase when youth bulges coincide with long-term per capita economic decline, high dependency ratios, expansions in higher education, or strong urban growth, the results suggest that the effect of youth bulges appears to be greater in the most autocratic regimes as well as in the most democratic states. *This may indicate that youth bulges provide greater opportunities in autocracies and greater motives in democracies.*

Youth Bulges, Terrorism, and Riots

The terrorism and riot data analyzed in my original paper are qualitatively inferior to the armed-conflict data and should be interpreted with caution.[35] Youth bulges generally seem to increase the risk of both forms of political violence. Furthermore, when youth bulges interact with long-term economic decline and with expansion in tertiary education, this significantly increases the risk of terrorism. Regime type, dependency ratios, and urbanization do not seem to be important contextual factors for the relationship between youth bulges and terrorism. Youth bulges appear to particularly increase the

BOX 6-2
The Significance of Youth Bulges

Countries with youth bulges making up at least 35 percent of the adult population run a risk of internal armed conflict that is 150 percent higher compared with the most developed countries if all other factors (including the
level of development and democracy) are the same. In 2000, fifteen- to
twenty-four-year-olds made up 17 percent or less of the total adult population
in almost all developed countries, the median being 15 percent. The same
year, forty-four developing countries experienced youth bulges of 35 percent
or above.

risk of rioting in societies with high dependency burdens, indicating that the
risk of such low-intensity violence may decrease when countries experience
declining fertility rates.

Conclusion

This chapter reports the findings of a recent empirical study suggesting that
youth bulges may provide both a motive and an opportunity for political violence.[36] Though bulges were found to increase the risk of internal armed conflict, terrorism, and rioting, the conditions when they are most volatile seem to
differ. Bulges seem to particularly increase the risk of terrorism and riots under
conditions of educational and economic stress, but bulges appear to provide
greater opportunities for armed conflict in autocracies and greater motives in
democracies. The following five policy implications have been identified on
the basis of this and other studies of youth bulges and political violence:

First, the importance of youth bulges in causing political violence is
expected to fade in most parts of the world over the next decades because of
declining fertility. But for states that will experience high youth shares for
years to come, especially in the Middle East, Africa, and parts of Asia, age
composition should still warrant some caution. Rapidly declining fertility
may provide opportunities for an economic bonus, possibly also contributing
to pacifying large youth cohorts.

Second, though fertility is also dropping in large parts of the Muslim
world, youth bulges currently pose a challenge to many Muslim governments.

In 2002, the *Arab Human Development Report* voiced concern over the widespread economic stagnation in the Arab world, and the consequences for the large youth groups.[37] A recent report on development cooperation as a means to fight terrorism concluded that "anti-terrorist development cooperation programming would be well advised to target the people who are most vulnerable to terrorist agitation, that is, well-educated young men who are frustrated about the lack of opportunities in the developing world."[38]

Third, a particular focus should be on providing employment or educational opportunities for youth in periods of economic decline, and on monitoring the employment situation of educated youth. Youth bulges may pose a greater security risk during times of economic decline and after expansion in higher education.

Fourth, limiting migration opportunities may increase the risk of violence in some countries with large youth bulges if this is not compensated for by increased domestic employment opportunities. Emigration may work as a safety valve in countries with large youth cohorts. In a recent survey, almost half of all Arab youth expressed a desire to emigrate as a result of concerns over job opportunities and education.[39] If migration opportunities are increasingly restricted without domestic initiatives in place to provide opportunities for youth, developing countries that previously relied on exporting surplus youth may experience increased pressures from youth bulges accompanied by a higher risk of political violence.

Fifth, more research is needed on the relationship between youth bulges and political violence, and on remedial policies. A particularly neglected aspect has been the role of these bulges in urban settings. Though the relationship between youth bulges, urbanization, and political violence does not show up strongly in global correlations, a more detailed analysis of youth and economic and social change in cities may provide important additional insights. Furthermore, no thorough review exists of the extent to which governments provide targeted programs aimed at muting the security risk posed by youth bulges, and whether such programs are effective.

Notes

1. Jack A. Goldstone, *Revolution and Rebellion in the Early Modern World* (University of California Press, 1991); Jack A. Goldstone, "Demography, Environment, and Security," in *Environmental Conflict,* ed. Paul F. Diehl and Nils Petter Gleditsch (Boulder, Colo.: Westview Press, 2001).

2. These are defined as large cohorts in the ages fifteen to twenty-four years relative to the total adult population.

3. Robert D. Kaplan, "The Coming Anarchy," *Atlantic Monthly,* February 1994, 46.

4. Fareed Zakaria, "The Roots of Rage," *Newsweek,* October 15, 2001, 14–33.

5. These results are reported in full in Henrik Urdal, "A Clash of Generations? Youth Bulges and Political Violence," *International Studies Quarterly* 50 (2006): 607–29.

6. Paul Collier, "Doing Well Out of War: An Economic Perspective," in *Greed & Grievance: Economic Agendas in Civil Wars,* ed. Mats Berdal and David M. Malone (Boulder, Colo.: Lynne Rienner, 2000).

7. Collier, "Doing Well Out of War," 94.

8. Nicholas Sambanis, "A Review of Recent Advances and Future Directions in the Quantitative Literature on Civil War," *Defense and Peace Economics* 13 (2002): 224.

9. Ted Robert Gurr, *Why Men Rebel* (Princeton University Press, 1970); Sambanis, "Review of Recent Advances," 223.

10. For examples, see Nazli Choucri, *Population Dynamics and International Violence: Propositions, Insights and Evidence* (Lexington, Mass.: Lexington Books, 1974); Richard G. Braungart, "Historical and Generational Patterns of Youth Movements: A Global Perspective," *Comparative Social Research* 7 (1984): 3–62; Goldstone, *Revolution and Rebellion;* and Goldstone, "Demography, Environment, and Security."

11. Colin H. Kahl, "Population Growth, Environmental Degradation, and State-Sponsored Violence: The Case of Kenya, 1991–93," *International Security* 23 (1998): 80–119.

12. Collier, "Doing Well Out of War."

13. Ibid.

14. Rachel Brett and Irma Specht, *Young Soldiers: Why They Choose to Fight* (Boulder, Colo.: Lynne Rienner, 2004).

15. Richard Easterlin, quoted in Diane J. Machunovich, "Relative Cohort Size: Source of a Unifying Theory of Global Fertility Transition?" *Population and Development Review* 26 (2000): 235–61; the quotation here is on p. 236.

16. Herbert Moller, "Youth as a Force in the Modern World," *Comparative Studies in Society and History* 10 (1968): 238–60; Choucri, *Population Dynamics and International Violence;* Braungart, "Historical and Generational Patterns"; Goldstone, *Revolution and Rebellion;* Goldstone, "Demography, Environment, and Security"; Richard P. Cincotta, Robert Engelman, and Daniele Anastasion, *The Security Demographic: Population and Civil Conflict after the Cold War* (Washington: Population Action International, 2003).

17. Onn Winckler, "The Demographic Dilemma of the Arab World: The Employment Aspect," *Journal of Contemporary History* 37 (2002): 617–36; the citation here is on p. 621.

18. Brynjar Lia, *Globalisation and the Future of Terrorism: Patterns and Predictions* (London: Routledge, 2005), 141.

19. Allen C. Kelley and Robert M. Schmidt, "Economic and Demographic Change: A Synthesis of Models, Findings, and Perspectives," in *Population Matters: Demographic Change, Economic Growth, and Poverty in the Developing World,* ed. Nancy Birdsall, Allen C. Kelley, and Steven W. Sinding (Oxford University Press, 2001).

20. Paul Collier and Anke Hoeffler, "Greed and Grievance in Civil War," *Oxford Economic Papers* 56 (2004): 563–95; the citation here is on p. 569.

21. Choucri, *Population Dynamics and International Violence,* 73.

22. Collier and Hoeffler, "Greed and Grievance."

23. Winckler, "Demographic Dilemma of the Arab World," 630.

24. Choucri, *Population Dynamics and International Violence,* 73.

25. Goldstone, "Demography, Environment, and Security," 95.

26. Lia, *Globalisation and the Future of Terrorism,* 145–46.

27. Håvard Hegre, Tanja Ellingsen, Scott Gates, and Nils Petter Gleditsch, "Toward a Democratic Civil Peace? Democracy, Political Change, and Civil War, 1816–1992," *American Political Science Review* 95 (2001): 33–48.

28. Goldstone, "Demography, Environment, and Security."

29. Lia, *Globalisation and the Future of Terrorism,* 147.

30. Ellen Brennan-Galvin, "Crime and Violence in an Urbanizing World," *Journal of International Affairs* 56 (2002): 123–46.

31. Lia, *Globalisation and the Future of Terrorism,* 141.

32. Goldstone, *Revolution and Rebellion;* Goldstone, "Demography, Environment, and Security."

33. For the model results, see Urdal, "Clash of Generations?" This analysis is based on the PRIO/Uppsala data set of conflicts with at least twenty-five battle deaths per year; see Nils Petter Gleditsch, Petter Wallensteen, Mikael Eriksson, Margareta Sollenberg, and Håvard Strand, "Armed Conflict 1946-2001: A New Dataset," *Journal of Peace Research,* 39 (2002): 615–37.

34. See Samuel P. Huntington, *The Clash of Civilizations and the Remaking of World Order* (New York: Simon & Schuster, 1996). There is, on the contrary, strong support for the suspicion that two authoritative civil war studies—James D. Fearon and David D. Laitin, "Ethnicity, Insurgency, and Civil War," *American Political Science Review,* 97 (2003): 75–90; and Collier and Hoeffler, "Greed and Grievance"—may have failed to find significant effects due to a flawed youth bulge measure. The State Failure Task Force Group found some effect of youth bulges on ethnic conflict; see Daniel C. Esty, Jack A. Goldstone, Ted Robert Gurr, Barbara Harff, Marc Levy, Geoffrey D. Dabelko, Pamela Surko, and Alan N. Unger, *State Failure Task Force Report: Phase II Findings* (McLean, Va.: Science Applications International, 1998).

35. The data were originally collected for the State Failure Task Force Project and are event (count) data collected from newspaper sources. For a discussion of data quality, see my original paper, Urdal, "Clash of Generations?"

36. The empirical study referred to is Urdal, "Clash of Generations?"

37. United Nations Development Program, *The Arab Human Development Report 2002: Creating Opportunities for Future Generations* (Amman, 2002), xv.

38. Timo Kivimäki, "Executive Summary," in *Development Cooperation as an Instrument in the Prevention of Terrorism,* ed. Timo Kivimäki (Copenhagen: Royal Danish Ministry of Foreign Affairs/Nordic Institute of Asia Studies, 2003).

39. United Nations Development Program, *Arab Human Development Report 2002.*

7

Embracing the Margins: Working with Youth amid War and Insecurity

MARC SOMMERS

> The growing size of a young generation among the general population in the Muslim world will magnify existing regime failures to find solutions to socio-economic and political problems. In the coming decades, these failures are certain to hasten the moment of regime crisis, causing eventual collapse in many cases with unknown consequences.
>
> — Graham E. Fuller, *The Youth Crisis in Middle Eastern Society*[1]

"RONALDO" WAS A four-year veteran of Liberia's civil war. He was first abducted in 2000 by Charles Taylor's army at the age of twelve years. His captors took him to a military camp, where he found many of his friends already there. They immediately warned him that "you have to be brave to survive." His subsequent bravery caught his general's eye, and Ronaldo soon became the general's houseboy and prize trainee. Ronaldo escaped but was later recaptured, eventually returning to his role in the general's service.

Once, when the general left their upcountry military base for consultations with Taylor in the capital, he made Ronaldo base commander in his stead. Soon thereafter, Ronaldo's military superiors ordered him to retreat to Monrovia with 3,600 soldiers and civilians under his command. The retreat lasted seventeen days and was labeled "Operation Dust to Dust" and "Man Moving, Man Dropping." These two names were employed to remind those under his command that "if anyone says, 'I'm tired, I can't make it,' you kill them." After reaching Monrovia, Ronaldo was immediately returned to the war front. He was fourteen years old at the time.[2]

Why have commanders been able to unlock the astounding resilience and potential of youth like Ronaldo while most governments and international institutions have not? It is an unfortunate irony of the current era that armed groups tend to value the versatility and resourcefulness of youth while civilian societies marginalize them. From suicide bombers and spies to field commanders and frontline warriors, there seems to be no end to what ever-younger boys and girls can do in the service of war and political violence.

At the same time, the social role of youth within war-affected states seems to be narrowing. Many are undereducated and migrating to cities and appear to be unemployed. There are also more of them in poor and unstable regions of Africa and the Middle East, where it often seems that nations do not know what to do with their own young people while armed groups keep discovering new ways to make use of them.

These twin perceptions of youth—of their expanding utility to armed groups and of their limited utility to civilian societies—have conspired to create an image of young people as menaces to their own communities. It is an image that has been promoted by some proponents of the "youth bulge," who view the rise in the proportion of young people in society, and their migration to urban areas, as a security threat. The post–September 11, 2001, world has further promoted the image of disaffected youth from certain areas of the world as potential terrorists.

Although there is no question that growing proportions of youth in unstable societies should be a priority concern, government and international policies may unintentionally be making the youth challenge worse. Youth are seen as dangerous in part because governments and international actors have misunderstood them and set youth priorities aside. Viewing young people through the youth bulge lens, moreover, can inaccurately fuel fearful connections between youth in certain areas of the world and terrorism.

This chapter argues that the perceived threat of youth to society is distorted and must be reassessed. It situates the youth bulge thesis in context, considers current policies that may be further marginalizing youth, reviews the central tenets of programming for marginalized youth, and concludes with recommendations aimed at reversing counterproductive policies and positively engaging youth to advance new policy directions.

The Youth Bulge in Context

We are promoting fear of the very people whom we should be positively partnering with: disadvantaged youth in poor and unstable nations. Though this fear can inspire harmful assumptions about young people and promote misguided policy responses, it is also partly based on demographic evidence underlying what is known as the youth bulge. Setting the youth bulge into context promises to provide a starting point for examining how it has supported certain policy directions that are unhelpful to development, peace building, and youth themselves.

Urdal has defined the youth bulge as "extraordinarily large youth cohorts relative to the adult population" of a nation.[3] Its particular significance stems from claims that youth bulges may cause political violence and even terrorism.[4] The perceived volatility of youth bulges is characterized by situations where there are "too many young men with not enough to do."[5] "Too many young men" is primarily described in ominous terms, because, it is asserted, "a large youth cohort intensifies and exacerbates most existing [societal] problems." Critical to arguments highlighting the youth bulge as a threat is the assertion that "young males are more prone to violence" than either older men or women.[6]

The youth bulge thesis, which reportedly originated with a geographer working for the Central Intelligence Agency in 1985,[7] has many advocates in the U.S. security community. Though the specter of hordes of unemployed young men, threatening peace and development and milling about in cities, was advanced by writers such as Robert D. Kaplan and Samuel P. Huntington a decade ago,[8] the employment of youth bulges as "a possible explanation for terrorism and increased global insecurity" dramatically increased following the September 11, 2001, attacks in the United States.[9] The U.S. Central Intelligence Agency's inspector general, John L. Helgerson, is among those who have employed the youth bulge thesis to signal a prime security threat. "The inability of states to adequately integrate youth populations is likely to perpetuate the cycle of political instability, ethnic wars, revolutions, and anti-government activities that already affects many countries. And a large proportion of youth will be living in cities, where opportunities will be limited."[10]

Much has been made of this highlighted demographic correlation between "too many young men" and instability, if not outright civil war and terrorism. Proponents consider it alarming,[11] while critics consider it alarmist.[12] Urdal considers the youth bulge as both "a blessing and a curse." It is a blessing because youth bulges can energize economies by expanding the pool of available labor. Youth bulges can become a curse if they occur within stagnant economies. Such a result, Urdal warns, "can be explosive."[13] Significantly, Urdal also argues that autocratic governance "acts to reduce the risk of conflict," while steps towards democratization "may substantially increase the risk of conflict in the Arab world."[14] This conclusion differs from that of others who argue that authoritarianism lies at the root of problems in the Middle East.[15]

Although the correlation between unusually high numbers of youth in a country and insecurity calls out for careful attention, the argument also requires contextualization. The following brief comments about those who connect the youth bulge with insecurity are intended to set the stage for the subsequent consideration of next steps.[16]

First, the argument is overly simplistic. The threat of instability and war is contained in a statistical correlation. Youth, and male youth in particular, are thought to be menacing mainly because there are "too many" of them. But a population demographic is not a cause of war; it only suggests some degree of probability. Ignoring other possible contributors to violent conflict runs the risk of distorting understandings of the causes of civil unrest and rebellion.

Second, it is not necessarily predictive. Even if the statistical connection between youth bulges and civil conflict is "extremely robust,"[17] the youth bulge does not explain the many situations where youth bulges do not lead to conflict. Moreover, most youth resist involvement in conflicts. As Barker and Ricardo note, "While the youth bulge argument is compelling, it is important to reaffirm that in any of these settings, only a minority of young men participate in conflicts. For example, the vast majority of young men, even those unemployed and out of school, were not involved in conflicts in Liberia and Sierra Leone."[18] Significantly, the youth bulge and insecurity literature neither highlights nor explains why most young men and women in unstable regions resist involvement in violence and terrorism.

Third, the depiction of youth is steadfastly negative. Youth are mainly described as threats to peace and stability, not potential forces for enhancing them. Goldstone illustrates this tendency when he states that "large youth cohorts are often drawn to new ideas and heterodox religions, challenging older forms of authority." This makes them "relatively easily mobilized for social or political conflicts" because most have limited family and career responsibilities.[19] The possibility that challenging older forms of authority might yield promising results, or be carried out through nonviolent means, is left out of the analysis. Positive youth involvement in confrontations against forces such as repression, corruption, exclusion, inequality, and injustice are not often mentioned by youth bulge and insecurity proponents. Sadly, the voices of youth resistance "are mostly in the shadows" while the actions of the violent minority "get the headlines and frighten the middle class."[20]

Fourth, despite statistics connecting young men to crime,[21] young men are not inherently violent. This is no small point, because the specter of an excess of young men threatening stability is a crucial component of the youth bulge and insecurity argument. Yet Rowe and his colleagues report that high levels of testosterone in the blood of adolescent males merely make them easily influenced by peers. Though they may copy delinquent behavior, the researchers also found that the high testosterone levels were "related to leadership rather than to antisocial behavior in boys who definitely did not have deviant peers."[22]

Fifth, the combination of the youth bulge and urbanization, which is often cited as particularly perilous because it may accelerate movement toward insecurity and political violence,[23] is overstated. Male youth may be flocking to cities in the developing world, and in Africa most particularly,[24] where their presence "is widely regarded as overwhelmingly negative, leading to crime, unrest and the spread of HIV/AIDS."[25] If it is assumed that young men are inherently violent, as claimed just above, then the cities to which they migrate in large numbers must therefore be explosive.

Yet in terms of security, youth migration to cities can be highly useful. Using the case of youth in Burundi's capital, Bujumbura, Ould-Abdallah notes that the cosmopolitanism of urban living can water down ethnic identification and threaten extremists because urban youth "unable to identify with an ethnic group . . . constitute living proof of the possibility of peaceful coexistence."[26] Moreover, excessive numbers of young men in African cities are nothing new. Many urban areas have been dominated by male youth almost since the colonial era. Colonial Nairobi, for example, had "an overwhelmingly male urban population," in part because British colonialists recruited men to work in Nairobi while prohibiting them from bringing their families along.[27]

Today, Kenya's capital is hardly a haven of serenity, and Kenya has been cited as a country "under a particular risk of experiencing armed conflict" due to the presence of the youth bulge and other risk factors.[28] Nonetheless, Nairobi and many other cities in countries with youth bulges can sensibly be considered more stable and less threatening than some projections might suggest. Additionally, reviewing recent conflicts in Africa suggests that urbanization's connection to violent conflict is not as strong as it is sometimes purported to be. Across the continent, from Burundi and Mozambique to Sierra Leone and Ethiopia, nearly every recent African conflict has arisen in rural, not urban, areas.

Sixth, the imagery that the youth bulge and insecurity argument can inspire—hordes of enraged young men in countries beyond the West—distorts actual realities. Young men living in particular nations are not predictively angry or dangerous. It is this image that Hendrixson forcefully attacks. She cites supporters of the youth bulge and insecurity thesis who assert that young men are "driven to violence by their very biology."[29] There is a racial cast to this argument, she contends, because the youth bulge threat has been personified as "a discontented, angry young man, almost always a person of color." Such young men are believed to constitute an "unpredictable, out-of-control force in the South generally, with Africa, the Middle East, and parts of Asia and Latin America all considered hot spots."[30]

Female youth, in turn, are presented as threatened by young men and threats themselves because of their "explosive fertility,"[31] which youth bulge and violence supporters directly connect to the "rise in numbers of young male terrorists."[32] The youth bulge and insecurity thesis, Hendrixson adds, is used to justify U.S. policies promoting population control (largely through programs for young women) and neoliberalism without examining whether such approaches support or compromise development. She concludes that such policies are "fraught with dangers"[33] and "punitive."[34]

Aiding Youth? Reflecting on the Current Record

If we looked at government policy in countries with youth bulges, would we know that their populations were increasingly dominated by youth? If we examined international agency policy in the same countries, could we tell that youth were demographically dominant? Probably not—although it is well known that youth constitute a massive proportion of developing nation populations, most governments and international aid agencies have been remarkably slow to fashion appropriate responses to their needs.

Most fortunately, this trend is beginning to change. Agencies such as the World Bank, the U.S. Agency for International Development (USAID), and the United Nations Development Program are among institutions that have recently released publications about youth, and youth facing unstable or conflict situations in particular, and how to support them.[35] A growing number of publications on this subject are emerging elsewhere as well.[36]

Before turning to trajectories arising from this still-new literature, it is useful to first examine aspects of the current record of international aid. What follows are four ways in which current policy appears to contribute to the creation of counterproductive results.

The first is linked to insufficient knowledge about the unintentional effects of development and reconstruction assistance. Though evaluating programs and projects is an issue attracting increasing attention, it is the quality of these evaluations that has been raised as a matter of particular concern. Recent contrasting information about USAID's evaluation record illustrates this tension between the quantity and quality of evaluations.

The USAID website highlights the fact that "USAID missions are evaluating their programs more often, enabling program managers to better understand how well USAID programs are working."[37] At the same time, however, a recent public discussion involving the former USAID administrator, Andrew Natsios, and the current deputy administrator, Carol Lancaster, highlighted the "inadequate" quality of USAID's evaluations. Natsios noted that USAID does not get "an objective analysis of what is really going on, whether the programs are working or not," while Lancaster stated that "everybody does a miserable job of evaluation" with regard to "figuring out whether we succeeded or not."[38]

The comments of Natsios and Lancaster suggest that more evaluation is not the answer if the underlying impact of initiatives in question remains unknown. Easterly, for example, argues that Western aid agencies remain largely unaccountable because they rarely seek feedback from their primary target group: the poor. He asks, "If the main problem with foreign aid is the lack of feedback from the poor themselves, and accountability to these same poor, then why not attack the problem directly?"[39] Uvin highlights the tendency of evaluations to emphasize broader, aggregate outcomes instead of pinpointing exactly which people received assistance. "Who exactly obtained the jobs, the land, the credits, or the training?" from assistance programs, he wonders. If such questions are not asked, international assistance earmarked to help the impoverished can instead expand the gap between rich and poor by further enriching the wealthy. As Uvin warns, "The same actions that promote positive aggregate outcomes may coincide with increased clientelism, corruption, inequality, exclusion, or insecurity for certain groups."[40]

The second way that well-intended policies can make matters worse is connected to precedent and speed. Field research in postwar Burundi indicated that "rebuilding damaged buildings, institutions, and authority systems without consideration of their geographic distribution runs the risk of simultaneously reinforcing structural inequities that were a root cause of civil war."[41] For government and international agencies, the most efficient way to rebuild a rural area may be to work in zones that have historically received the lion's share of assistance. These "favored" zones are generally the most accessible, already have structures and institutions that can be quickly reconstructed, and house educated elites that can facilitate the process. Such actions discriminate against the majority of rural residents who reside in "neglected" zones. The result may be an unintentional expansion of existing inequalities and a possible signal, in the eyes of the poor, neglected majority, of a government office's or aid agency's support for such inequalities. This sort of well-intended postwar peace-building assistance can instead help set the stage for "widespread discontent and possible violence."[42]

The third way that policies can generate counterproductive outcomes is linked to a preference for international agencies in some countries to concentrate postwar efforts in rural areas. The tendency is illuminated by the author's 2005 fieldwork in Liberia, where many international donors were found to be earmarking their assistance for rural areas while support for integrating former combatants, most of whom lived in the capital city, was widely considered inadequate. One aid official supporting rural investment stated that "the way forward for youth is agriculture, whether they like it or not." Drawing urban youth back to their rural villages of origin was one purpose of rural-focused programming. At the same time, there is little evidence that urban migrant youth in Africa return to reside in their former rural homes.[43]

The fourth way that international aid policies may produce unfortunate consequences is suggested by recent evidence that gender policies favoring girls and women may be dangerously misguided. Correia and Bannon have argued that gender policies since the 1970s have focused on "the ways in which men exercise power over and dominate women." But they argue that this is only half of the entire picture: "Gender is also about the way social structures and authority give men power over other men, thus resulting in their marginalization, discrimination, and subordination."[44] Male youth are frequently at the receiving end of this uneven relationship, and it can be a cause of conflict.

Male youth—victims of exploitation and control by older men and the state—are often unable to own land, marry, and shed the youth label to become adults. Thus, male youth may be attracted to war because of "the promise of being able to marry, which they otherwise could not do" and to avoid the frustration and humiliation caused by "their inability to meet societal expectations of manhood."[45] Correia and Bannon further warn that

> unrealistic, unattainable, and rigid norms of conduct and expectations placed on men contribute not only to disparities and inequities on women, but to men's discontent—and when these expectations are combined with factors such as racism, adultism, and weak states—to the underdevelopment and destruction of nations and regions, and even to terrorism.[46]

Responses to unstable countries with youth bulge demographics that recommend explicit responses to the needs of women but no corollary recommendations for supporting men may make a dire situation for young men and the larger society much worse.[47]

Youth as Resources for Stability and Growth

The strength and the weakness of the youth bulge and insecurity argument is that it highlights challenges confronting states with disproportionately large youth populations. It both spotlights an important issue involving youth while overshadowing the realities that youth face. This imbalance has invited depictions of youth as dark security threats, which Kaplan memorably illuminated in his description of young men in urban West Africa as "out of school, unemployed, loose molecules in an unstable social fluid that threatened to ignite."[48]

Given the fear and disquiet that youth can inspire, a central component of the youth challenge involves providing a balanced, accurate picture of youth themselves. This has proven difficult for the youth bulge literature to present, partly because it contains few or no interviews with the young people that the authors are so worried about. Left without a voice, restive, unemployed young men from unstable regions serve to embody the threats of violence and even terrorism in the West without securing a chance to explain how things look from their perspective.

In addition to being characterized as threats, youth are also highlighted as victims (together with children), most prominently in Graça Machel's report *The Impact of Armed Conflict on Children* and her follow-up study.[49] Both perspectives have been challenged by growing evidence that war-affected youth are remarkably resilient actors in improving their own lives.[50] There are increasing calls for positioning youth as primary social and economic resources for peace building and stability instead of "assuming that young people are themselves the problem."[51]

International agency work with at-risk youth, particularly those in poor, unstable, and conflict-affected nations, remains new. Its strength lies in its advocacy for engaging directly with youth and addressing their needs. Inclusion and quality concerns remain persistent challenges. There is an apparent tendency to include more higher-class (and mostly male) youth than members of the marginalized majority, and more male youth than female youth. The field is also plagued by insufficient numbers of good-quality youth program evaluations, which have made it difficult to determine which youth programming approaches are even reasonably effective.[52]

At the same time, certain issues repeatedly surface as central to working successfully with youth. Young people want access to education, training, and work. Many already work in informal economies, are small-time entrepreneurs, and seek access to capital.[53] Direct engagement with youth in program development and evaluation is widely considered as central to successful youth programming. Because youth have a myriad of issues confronting them, holistic programs that address many concerns (for example, basic education, vocational training, and health concerns) are thought to have a higher chance for yielding a positive impact among young people.[54]

This is precisely the approach adopted by the "two most powerful forces of youth mobilization [that] have emerged in recent years—Islam and Christian Pentecostalism."[55] In addition to providing spiritual and moral guidance, security, structure, and community, these two religious groups address grievances that youth regularly highlight, particularly regarding education and employment.[56] Religious programs often draw from the advantage created by states that are unable or (much more likely, it often appears) not interested in or afraid of engaging with youth. As Singer suggests, many Muslim madrassa schools "also provide social welfare services, such as free food to poor students. They gain students and popularity by filling the state's void."[57]

Taken together, the thrust of these approaches to the needs of young people is based on the contention that directly engaging members of the poor, socially marginalized, disenfranchised, alienated, and extremely frustrated youth majority with participatory, proactive, youth-centered measures is the only way to promote stability and growth for youth and the greater society that they may demographically dominate. This is obviously a considerable challenge in countries with huge youth populations—no program can address the needs of a multitude of youth in need. But it is also apparent that the sheer size of youth populations makes positive engagement with them essential to the promotion of lasting peace and development.

Recommendations for Learning and Action

A necessary component of successful security, governance, and development policy for war-affected and other insecure nations is an effective method for including and engaging with youth. As reviewed in this chapter, there is a need to reverse trends toward viewing youth in negative terms, carrying out actions that unintentionally worsen situations facing youth, and inadequately evaluating youth programs. The concluding section offers a general approach and specific recommendations for addressing these concerns and developing a policy framework.

Creating Choices

"Julius" and "James" were among the former soldiers I interviewed in Eastern Congo in 2005. Tired of war and enticed by the promise of peacetime life, they left the bush and entered a demobilization program. But troubles soon followed. The money they received from the program did not last long. They searched for work but, given their wartime experience, no one would hire them. "We don't want to become beggars or thieves," Julius explained, "but with no job and no money, how are we going to live?"

Frustrated with his marginal social status and increasingly desperate economic situation, James reminisced about life in the military. "When I had a gun," he recalled, "life was more interesting. I could have anything—money, food, girls—any time I wanted." But Julius added that dignified civilian work was what they now sought. "Even if you give me twenty dollars," he explained, "it won't help me because I didn't work for it. But if I make my own money, I'd spend it with intelligence." After a few short weeks of civilian life, with little money and few options, desperation was setting in. "Without a job," James speculated, "at some point we're going to return to the military. We have no choice."

We have no choice. Working with young people in poor and unstable areas hinges on providing them with viable, appropriate choices. They are often justifiably frustrated with their situation and the regime they must endure, feeling stuck for reasons that are entirely sensible. War also changes lives. Youth are often pitched into roles that they traditionally are not expected to perform. Many marry early, become entrepreneurs, migrate to cities, create youth-centered networks, and have no intention of ever returning to cultural roles or rural homes that they may view as confining.

Wars alter youth lives in ways that leaders and institutions may find difficult to accept. Indeed, there is a tendency for them to mark territory before knowing it well. This is underscored by the use of the term "reintegration" to characterize a common objective of postwar programming, particularly for former soldiers. As a USAID publication states, "The problem of reintegrating former combatants into community life is a standard feature of post-conflict settings."[58] Yet "reintegration" implies some sort of return to how preconflict communities operated, the sort of thing that many youth seek to avoid. Youth often emerge from war with new skills, experiences, and identities, and they may have no interest in a return to the past. Employing "reintegration" as a conceptual starting point for engaging with war-affected youth is thus inappropriate because it creates an expectation that many young people do not want and may resist. "Integration" is a far more broadly applicable and appropriate term.

The task before both governments and nongovernmental institutions is to learn from youth about their lives and what they seek *before* employing stopgap or prefabricated measures, and then work with youth to build a positive future. This sounds unrealistic: There are too many young people with too many problems to reasonably deal with. However, the opposite is also true: There are far too many young people in unstable areas to ignore.

A prominent challenge confronting nations with youth-dominated populations is that their governments' policies are rarely youth centered. Indeed, some governments of nations with swelling urban youth populations view them as something equivalent to, in the words of a former Tanzanian minister for labor and youth development, "anti-socials."[59] The logic of survival and the search for a dignified existence often puts youth at loggerheads with governments yearning to preserve a social status quo where youth are subordinate. But as the stories of Ronaldo, Julius, and James illustrate, war and instability can change all that. Meanwhile, government attitudes toward youth in cities where many young people migrate "might not extend much beyond a sneer and a curled lip."[60] This is not, to say the least, a useful starting point for productively engaging with large numbers of youthful citizens.

Ten Recommendations

The problem with the youth bulge lies not in its accuracy but how it is employed. If it is used to promote security from youth instead of security for them, then it will likely advance insecurity. If it is used to support (and not reform) regimes featuring policies and actions that both constrain and repress young people and demonstrate exclusion, injustice, inequality, corruption, and nepotism, then it will probably exacerbate existing youth frustrations with that regime. The following ten recommendations suggest ways to positively and productively engage with young people in countries where most are poor, frustrated, and alienated.

First, prioritize "youth bulge" countries. More youth should mean more investment for them, and it should be carried out in a way that is youth-centered, participatory, and empowering.

Second, stop making it worse. Institute lessons learned about counterproductive aid policies. Avoid employing a security framework toward youth because it runs the risk of further alienating already alienated youth.

Third, create a learning environment. Employ evaluators with emphatically independent, unbiased perspectives and evaluation techniques that do not aim to please their employers but, instead, search deeply into the broader context of a program's impact, whether it is positive, negative, or negligible, and how long the impact might last. Make the program accountable not to government and other elite agendas but to the target group; in this case, poor youth. Carry out baseline assessments of youth lives, learn about how youth view their challenges and place in society, and examine government and economic conditions in advance of programming involving youth. Explore why most youth resist engagement in violence. Invite youth to assist in evaluation work.[61]

Fourth, develop a national youth policy and make its implementation a high priority. The process should be inclusive of excluded youth voices and concerns. As Richards urges, "Basic requirements are a national youth policy and a serious budget to allow, among other things, experimentation in youth activities designed to foster social cohesion."[62]

Fifth, highlight youth inclusion as a test of democratization and good governance. Large numbers of marginalized youth in many developing countries challenge representative governance because they tend to be inadequately represented in both government and civil society and may not vote in large numbers. Widely recognized youth leaders are often educated elites whose ability to represent and advocate for the needs and views of the marginalized youth majority is questionable. Many youth may be both victims of government misconduct and passionate advocates for responsive, accessible, and democratic governments, making them essential partners for political reform.

Sixth, expect to fail (at first). Working with alienated, disenfranchised young people is challenging. Given the still-weak evaluation record of youth programs, it is not entirely clear what will succeed. Search out and admit to existing failures, keeping in mind Vartan Gregorian's warning that "if you don't concede you have failed, everything is suspect."[63] Create well-resourced, participatory, adaptable programs for youth that can adjust to changing conditions and problems surfacing from the monitoring process.

Seventh, aim for the marginalized youth majority. Ensure that investments in youth are balanced by gender and directed at the particular needs and concerns of male and female youth. This should include understanding and addressing the near-invisibility of female youth and the emasculation of male youth in the many societies where this persists. Further empowering adult leaders is very likely counterproductive. Given a chance, many youth may seek to transform their cultural, social, and economic roles. Design strategic approaches for identifying which youth should be targeted for programming, but highlight the needs of the marginalized majority.

Eighth, work with youth where they already are. Youth in cities may not be what governments and international institutions seek. Yet young people have good reasons to be in urban areas. Their presence might be a strategy for diversifying household investments, a preparatory stage before marriage, a location of choice, or a combination of these and many other factors. Large urban youth populations are a reality that must be accepted, in part because most urban youth are difficult if not impossible to move.

Ninth, network with and learn from those already working with youth. This would include religious organizations, which are often the only groups working effectively with marginalized youth.

Tenth, employ holistic approaches. Work with youth to design programs that address the most important of their concerns, which tend to include provisions for vocational training, education, and microfinance, while incorporating other needs (for example, health, basic skills, and peaceful conflict resolution).

Living in the Age of Youth

Whether we accept it or not, we are living in the age of youth. Today, the size of the youth population "is larger both numerically and proportionally than it has ever been." Nearly half of all humans are under the age of twenty-five years, a billion are between ten and nineteen, and "with declining fertility in most of the world, there will likely never be in human history a youth cohort this large again."[64]

Yet this age of youth is contained within a climate of fear. The security orientation of most youth bulge and insecurity advocates helps to concretize the source of this fear: young men, particularly those in the Middle East and Africa. Mixing fear with youth bulge statistics is a counterproductive cocktail because it invites distortions of critical issues and distances government and nongovernmental institutions from youth, making it much tougher to discover and employ viable solutions.

The challenge confronting the global community, then, is how to accept and positively respond to the challenges and potential that young people embody. This is not going to be easy, because too many youth in developing countries occupy the ironic position of dominating societies demographically while seeing themselves as social outcasts. Providing more jobs, training, credit, and education for young people is a necessary step, because investments in youth are generally far too low in poor and war-affected nations.

But it is also likely insufficient, because the presence of a substantial proportion of a society who consider themselves to be outsiders creates important implications for governance, development, and security policy. Devising an appropriate response, in short, calls for getting government and nongovernmental agencies to think about youth in a different way—less as "leaders of tomorrow" and more as excluded citizens and essential partners.

Notes

1. Graham E. Fuller, *The Youth Crisis in Middle Eastern Society: Brief Paper* (Clinton Township, Mich.: Institute for Social Policy and Understanding, 2004), 12.

2. This was drawn from a firsthand interview with a former child soldier in Monrovia, Liberia.

3. Henrik Urdal, *The Devil in the Demographics: The Effect of Youth Bulges on Domestic Armed Conflict, 1950–2000,* Social Development Papers: Conflict Prevention & Reconstruction Paper 14 (Washington: World Bank, 2004), 1.

4. Ibid.

5. Richard P. Cincotta, Robert Engelman, and Daniele Anastasion, *The Security Demographic: Population and Civil Conflict after the Cold War* (Washington: Population Action International, 2003), 44.

6. Graham E. Fuller, *The Youth Factor: The New Demographics of the Middle East and the Implications for U.S. Policy,* Analysis Paper 3, Saban Center for Middle East Policy (Brookings, 2003), 2.

7. Anne Hendrixson, "The 'Youth Bulge': Defining the Next Generation of Young Men as a Threat to the Future," *DifferenTakes,* Winter 2003, 2 (http://popdev.hampshire.edu/projects/dt/pdfs/DifferenTakes_19.pdf).

8. Robert D. Kaplan, *The Ends of the Earth: A Journey at the Dawn of the 21st Century* (New York: Random House, 1996). Samuel P. Huntington, *The Clash of Civilizations and the Remaking of the World Order* (New York: Simon & Schuster, 1996). Also see Robert D. Kaplan, "The Coming Anarchy," *Atlantic Monthly,* February 1994, 44–76.

9. Ian Bannon, "Foreword," in *Devil in the Demographics,* by Urdal; Anne Hendrixson, "Angry Young Men, Veiled Young Women: Constructing a New Population Threat," Corner House Briefing 34, December 2004, 2 (www.thecornerhouse.org.uk/pdf/briefing/34veiled.pdf).

10. The author was chairman of the U.S. government's National Intelligence Council when he drafted this article. John L. Helgerson, "The National Security Implications of Global Demographic Change," April 2002, 3–4 (www.au.af.mil/au/awc/awcgate/cia/helgerson2.htm).

11. For example, Helgerson, "National Security Implications."

12. For example, Hendrixson, "The 'Youth Bulge'"; Hendrixson, "Angry Young Men, Veiled Young Women."

13. Urdal, *Devil in the Demographics,* 16.

14. Ibid., 17.

15. See Fuller, *Youth Factor,* 35.

16. In this chapter, those who highlight correlations between the youth bulge and some combination of insecurity, instability, political violence, warfare, and terrorism are referred to as "supporters" or "proponents" of the "youth bulge and insecurity" thesis.

17. Urdal, *Devil in the Demographics,* 16.

18. Gary Barker and Christine Ricardo, "Young Men and the Construction of Masculinity in Sub-Saharan Africa," in *The Other Half of Gender: Men's Issues in Development,* ed. Ian Bannon and Maria C. Correia (Washington: World Bank, 2006), 181.

19. Jack A. Goldstone, "Population and Security: How Demographic Change Can Lead to Violent Conflict," *Journal of International Affairs* 56, no. 1 (Fall 2002): 10–11.

20. Gary Barker, *Dying to Be Men: Youth, Masculinity and Social Exclusion* (London: Routledge, 2005), 157.

21. Cincotta, Engelman, and Anastasion, *Security Demographic,* 44.

22. Richard Rowe, Barbara Maughan, Carol M. Worthman, E. Jane Costello, and Adrian Angold, "Testosterone, Antisocial Behavior, and Social Dominance in Boys: Pubertal Development and Biosocial Interaction," *Biological Psychiatry* 55, no. 5 (2004): 550.

23. See Helgerson, "National Security Implications of Global Demographic Change"; Office of Conflict Management and Mitigation, *Youth and Conflict: A Toolkit for Intervention* (Washington: U.S. Agency for International Development, 2005).

24. Ernest Harsch, "African Cities under Strain: Initiatives to Improve Housing, Services, Security and Governance," *Africa Recovery* 15, no. 12 (2001): 1–9.

25. Michi Ebata, Valeria Izzi, Alexandra Lendon, Eno Ngjela, Peter Sampson, and Jane Lowicki-Zucca, *Youth and Violent Conflict: Society and Development in Crisis?* (New York: Bureau for Crisis Prevention, United Nations Development Program, 2006), 28.

26. Ahmedou Ould-Abdallah, *Burundi on the Brink 1993–95: A UN Special Envoy Reflects on Preventive Diplomacy* (Washington: U.S. Institute of Peace Press, 2000), 21.

27. J. Roger Kurtz, *Urban Obsessions, Urban Fears: The Postcolonial Kenyan Novel* (Trenton, N.J.: Africa World Press, 1998), 78.

28. Urdal, *Devil in the Demographics,* 17.

29. Hendrixson, "Angry Young Men, Veiled Young Women," 10.

30. Ibid., 8.

31. Ibid., 2.

32. Ibid., 11.

33. Ibid., 11–12.

34. Ibid., 3.

35. World Bank, *Children and Youth: A Framework for Action* (Washington: World Bank, 2005); Office of Conflict Management and Mitigation, *Youth and Conflict;* Ebata and others, *Youth and Violent Conflict.*

36. Yvonne Kemper, *Youth in War-to-Peace Transitions: Approaches of International Organizations* (Berlin: Berghof Research Center for Constructive Conflict Management, 2005); Jane Lowicki and Allison Pillsbury, *Untapped Potential: Adolescents Affected by Armed Conflict. A Review of Programs and Policies* (New York: Women's Commission for Refugee Women and Children, 2000); Jesse Newman, *Protection through Participation: Young People Affected by Forced Migration and Political Crisis,* Refugee Studies Centre Working Paper 20 (Oxford: Refugee Studies Centre, Oxford University, 2005); Marc Sommers, *Youth: Care and Protection of Children in Emergencies. A Field Guide* (Westport, Conn.: Save the Children Federation, 2001) (www.ineesite.org/assess/field_guide_

sommers.pdf); Marc Sommers, *Youth and Conflict: A Brief Review of Available Literature* (Washington: Education Development Center and U.S. Agency for International Development, 2006); Cathryn L. Thorup and Sheila Kinkade, *What Works in Youth Engagement in the Balkans* (Baltimore and Skopje: International Youth Foundation and Balkan Children and Youth Foundation, 2005); United Nations Center for Human Settlements (UN-Habitat), *Strategy Paper on Urban Youth in Africa: A Focus on the Most Vulnerable Groups: A Safer Cities Perspective* (New York: Safer Cities Program, United Nations Human Settlements Program, 2004); United Nations Children's Fund (UNICEF), *Adolescence: A Time That Matters* (New York: UNICEF, 2002); UNICEF, *Working for and with Adolescents: Some UNICEF Examples (Selected Case Studies)* (New York: Adolescent Development and Participation Unit, UNICEF, 2002) (www.usaid.gov/press/frontlines/fl_dec05/development/htm).

37. U.S. Agency for International Development, "Frontlines: Inside Development: Increase in Aid Evaluations Improves Ability to Get Results," 1 (www.usaid.gov/press/frontlines/fl_dec05/development.htm).

38. Center for Global Development, *Evaluation Gap Update: May 2006* (Washington, 2006), 2 (www.cgdev.org/section/initiatives/_active/evalgap/eupdate?print=1).

39. William Easterly, *The White Man's Burden: Why the West's Efforts to Aid the Rest Have Done So Much Ill and So Little Good* (New York: Penguin Press, 2006), 380.

40. Peter Uvin, *Aiding Violence: The Development Enterprise in Rwanda* (West Hartford, Conn.: Kumarian, 1998), 154.

41. Marc Sommers, *It Always Rains in the Same Place First: Geographic Favoritism in Rural Burundi,* Africa Program Issue Briefing 1 (Washington: Woodrow Wilson International Center for Scholars, 2005), 1 (www.wilsoncenter.org/topics/docs/IB001.pdf).

42. Ibid., 5.

43. Osita Ogbu and Gerrishon Ikiara, "The Crisis of Urbanization in Sub-Saharan Africa," *Courier,* January–February 1995, 52–59; Marc Sommers, *Urbanization, War, and Africa's Youth at Risk: Towards Understanding and Addressing Future Challenges* (Washington: Basic Education and Policy Support, Activity and Creative Associates International, 2003) (www.beps.net/publications/BEPS-UrbanizationWarYouthatRisk-.pdf). Also see Sommers, *Youth and Conflict,* 4–5, for further examination of this issue.

44. Maria C. Correia and Ian Bannon, "Gender and Its Discontents: Moving to Men-Streaming Development," in *Other Half of Gender,* ed. Bannon and Correia, 245.

45. Ibid., 251.

46. Ibid., 259.

47. See Cincotta, Engelman, and Anastasion, *Security Demographic,* 15–16.

48. Kaplan, *Ends of the Earth,* 16.

49. The original study: Graça Machel, *The Impact of Armed Conflict on Children* (Geneva: United Nations, 1996) (www.unicef.org/graca/a51-306_en.pdf). The follow-up study: Graça Machel, *The Impact of War on Children: A Review of the Progress since the 1996 United Nations Report on the Impact of Armed Conflict on Children* (London: Hurst & Co., 2001).

50. See Jo Boyden and Joanna de Berry, eds., *Children and Youth on the Front Line: Ethnography, Armed Conflict and Displacement* (Oxford: Berghahn Books, 2004).

51. Ebata and others, *Youth and Violent Conflict,* 74.

52. Sommers, *Youth and Conflict,* 24–25.

53. Geetha Nagarajan, *Microfinance, Youth and Conflict: Emerging Lessons and Issues,* Micronote 4 (Washington: Chemonics International, 2005), 1–2; Sommers, *Urbanization, War, and Africa's Youth at Risk,* 13–14.

54. See Office of Conflict Management and Mitigation, *Youth and Conflict;* Barry Sesnan, Graham Wood, Marina L. Anselme, and Ann Avery, "Skills Training for Youth," *Forced Migration Review,* May 2004, 33–35 (www.fmreview.org/FMRpdfs/FMR20/FMR2016.pdf).

55. Ebata and others, *Youth and Violent Conflict,* 29.

56. Ibid.; Sommers, *Urbanization, War, and Africa's Youth at Risk,* 14–15.

57. P. W. Singer, *Time for the Hard Choices: The Dilemmas Facing U.S. Policy towards the Islamic World,* Brookings Project on U.S. Policy Towards the Islamic World, Working Paper 1 (Brookings, 2002), 8.

58. U.S. Agency for International Development, *Community-Focused Reintegration* (Washington: U.S. Agency for International Development, 2006), 5.

59. Marc Sommers, "Young, Male and Pentecostal: Urban Refugees in Dar es Salaam, Tanzania," *Journal of Refugee Studies* 14, no. 4 (2001): 364.

60. Ibid.

61. Or even become lead evaluators; see Jane Lowicki, "Beyond Consultation: In Support of More Meaningful Adolescent Participation," *Forced Migration Review,* October 2002, 33–35 (www.fmreview.org/FMRpdfs/FMR15/fmr15.14.pdf).

62. Paul Richards, "Young Men and Gender in War and Postwar Reconstruction: Some Comparative Findings from Liberia and Sierra Leone," in *Other Half of Gender,* ed. Bannon and Correia, 215.

63. David Leonhardt, "The Buffett Memorial Column," *New York Times,* June 28, 2006.

64. Barker, *Dying to Be Men,* 11.

8

The Role of Leadership in Overcoming Poverty and Achieving Security in Africa

ROBERT I. ROTBERG

TODAY THERE IS a widespread recognition in sub-Saharan Africa that the continent's earlier leaders, and some of those still in charge, erred by attempting to repeal the fundamental laws of economics, by grabbing wealth for themselves and their clients, and by pretending that their antidemocratic instincts were culturally sanctioned—that Africans preferred autocracy to real democratic practice. There are still a few throwbacks; several contemporary heads of state continue to be mired in the old ways. But whereas Africans several decades ago accepted misrule, nowadays Africans revile the excesses of past and present leaders and expect their heads of state and heads of government to perform to a global standard.

Vigorous opposition movements now provide accountability in many formerly powerful single-ruler states. Major regime changes in Ghana and Senegal; the denial of third presidential terms to Olusegun Obasanjo in Nigeria, Frederick Chiluba in Zambia, and Bakili Muluzi in Malawi; and Thabo Mbeki's pledge not to seek a third presidential term in South Africa confirm a new wave of responsible leadership approaches, despite contrary evidence from Namibia and serious lapses in Equatorial Guinea, Eritrea, Ethiopia, Togo, and Zimbabwe. From Liberia to Kenya, and from Mozambique to Mauritania, Africans now expect their leaders to be more participatory and transparent, and much more responsive to citizens and citizens' needs than ever before. Recent Afrobarometer results voice democratic African aspirations and impatience at anything less than full participation in their national political processes.[1]

According to such attitudinal surveys, Africans desire good government and good leadership, as do citizens everywhere who battle bureaucratic obstacles and crave services and opportunities that are scarce or nonexistent. But it is only the fortunate few, who live in the stable, peaceful, and better-run states (for example, Botswana), who can go about their daily business with expectations of order, fairness, consistency, and predictability. Too many still fear predation and corruption. Too many anticipate that faucets will go dry, lights flicker and dim, stores run out of maize meal and cooking oil, gas pumps become empty, roads fill with potholes, and government offices lose the permits or approval stamps necessary for everyday transactions. That is the rough-and-ready regrettable lot of Africans in the many countries still run by dictators, military juntas, guided democrats, and corrupted democrats. In those places (fewer than before, but still too numerous), good governance still remains an aspiration rather than a right or an expectation.

Effective leaders, themselves concerned about and anxious to ensure well-run states, are the first guarantors of good governance. The number of those leaders is gradually increasing in sub-Saharan Africa. It is evident, too, that only capable leaders determined to root out corruption, strengthen the rule of law, and invigorate national bureaucracies can truly transform intention into performance and can supply reasonable measures of good governance to their citizens. Only leaders with a clear vision and the determination to deliver positive value to their citizens can overcome the institutional weaknesses and temptations of power and enrichment that have enmeshed weaker or more susceptible African leaders in webs of cavalier or conscious malfeasance.

Overcoming poverty and increasing security take the same leadership skills. Indeed, nowhere else is committed leadership so critical to the achievement of prosperity and stability as it is in Africa. The smaller, the more fragile the state, the more good leadership matters. That is, in situations where human resource capacity is limited, effective and visionary leadership is that much more fundamental and decisive. Because Africa has many more nation-states, many more weak ones, and many more landlocked and thus constrained ones than any other continent, good leadership makes a considerable difference. Indeed, Africa has not distinguished itself over the years in its leadership attainments. There have been too few Seretse Khamas and too many Idi Amins and Mobutu Sese Sekos. Africa remains poor and insecure largely because of its immense leadership deficit.

Leadership in the African arena determines whether states deliver effective political goods to their citizens. Political goods are those intangible and hard-to-quantify claims that citizens once made on sovereigns and now make on states. They encompass expectations, conceivably obligations, inform the local political culture, and together give content to the social contract between ruler and ruled that is at the core of regime/government and citizenry interactions.

There is a hierarchy of political goods.[2] None is as critical as the supply of security, especially human security. Individuals alone, almost exclusively in special or particular circumstances, can attempt to make themselves secure. Or groups of individuals can band together to organize and purchase goods or services that maximize their sense of security. Traditionally, and usually, however, individuals and groups cannot easily or effectively substitute privately arranged security for the full spectrum of publicly provided security. The state's prime function is to provide that political good of security—to prevent cross-border invasions and infiltrations, and any loss of territory; to eliminate domestic threats to or attacks upon the national order and social structure; to prevent crime and any related dangers to domestic human security; and to enable citizens to resolve their differences with the state and with their fellow inhabitants without recourse to arms or other forms of physical coercion.[3]

The delivery of a range of other desirable political goods becomes possible when a reasonable measure of security has been sustained. Modern states (as successors to sovereigns) provide predictable, recognizable, systematized methods of adjudicating disputes and regulating both the norms and the prevailing mores of a particular society or polity. The essence of that political good usually implies codes and procedures that together constitute an enforceable body of law, security of property and inviolable contracts, an effective judicial system, and a set of norms that legitimate and validate the values embodied in a local version of the rule of law.

Political freedom is another critical political good, as is economic opportunity. The former enables citizens to participate in society and influence the conduct of their nation-state. Political competition is implicit, as are freedom of expression and freedom of assembly. Respect for human rights is essential. Freely held elections are included under this political good, but an election is a reflection and not the only embodiment of this political good.

Economic opportunity permits individuals to maximize their personal entrepreneurial instincts within an effectively regulated economic environment. It creates a beneficent fiscal and institutional framework. For this political good to be realized, the nation-state must create macroeconomic and microeconomic conditions conducive to growth, usually including stable monetary arrangements, a satisfactory central banking system, and a national currency.

Other political goods typically supplied by states and expected by their citizenries (although privatized forms are possible) include medical and health care (at varying levels and costs); schools and educational instruction (of various kinds and levels); roads, railways, harbors, and other physical infrastructure—the arteries of commerce; communications networks; space for the flowering of civil society; and methods of regulating the sharing of the environmental commons. Better-run nation-states also pay attention to gender representativeness, and they show that respect through officeholder numbers and empowerment.

Together, this bundle of political goods, roughly rank-ordered, establishes a set of criteria according to which modern nation-states may be judged on their performance. The leaders of African states overwhelmingly determine the flowering or diminution of good governance according to these criteria.

Strong states obviously perform well across these categories and separately with respect to each. Weak states show a mixed profile, fulfilling expectations in some areas and performing poorly in others. The more poorly weak states perform, criterion by criterion, the weaker they become, and the more that weakness tends to edge toward failure; hence the subcategory of weakness that is termed failing. Many failed states flunk each test outlined above, and poverty and insecurity follow. All cases of internal violence in Africa (and elsewhere) are associated directly with failure and the propensity to fail. Yet violence alone does not condition failure, and the absence of violence does not necessarily imply that the state in question has not failed. It is necessary to judge the extent to which an entire failing or failed profile is less or more than its component parts.

Strong states unquestionably control their territories and deliver a full range and high quality of political goods to their citizens. They perform well according to such indicators as gross domestic product (GDP) per capita, the United Nations Development Program's Human Development Index, Transparency International's Corruption Perception Index, and the criteria found in Freedom House's *Freedom of the World Report*. Strong states offer high levels of security from political and criminal violence, ensure political freedom and civil liberties, and create environments conducive to the growth of economic opportunity. The rule of law prevails. Judges are independent. Road networks are well maintained. Telephones work. Snail mail and e-mail both arrive quickly. Schools, universities, and students flourish. Hospitals and clinics serve patients effectively. And so on. Overall, strong states are places of enviable peace and order. Strong states represent the aspirations of nearly all Africans (other than those who live in Botswana, Mauritius, and South

Africa and who enjoy such benefits already). But those aspirations are too often achieved in the breach—hence poverty and insecurity.

Most of all and easiest to demonstrate, the leadership factor has determined whether millions of innocent civilians have lost their lives—3 million in Congo, 2 million in Sudan, 2 million in Angola, and now at least 200,000 in genocidal Darfur.

Likewise, human agency has determined whether Africans enjoy good educational and health outcomes and increasing or decreasing standards of living. Structure is less important than leadership. That is why Botswana, once dirt poor, is now rich. But the case is even more strikingly made in Mauritius, once a poor sugar-producing island and now one of the world's fastest-growing plural societies thanks to innovative and honest leadership, collaboration across sectors and parties, and striking trade openness.

At the other extreme is Zimbabwe, where massive leadership deficiencies have led in the past seven years to negative growth of at least 40 percent, a plunge of GDP per capita from $800 in 1999 to $250 in 2006, inflation that in 2007 soared over 1,600 percent a year, and a massive currency depreciation and forced revaluation. Along the way, 80 percent of Zimbabweans have become unemployed, a quarter of the total population of 12 million has fled to South Africa and Botswana, HIV/AIDS has become far more of a scourge than before, life expectancies have plummeted into the low thirties, and—according to authoritative studies—the country has now fallen backward to 1953 economic levels of performance.[4] The World Food Program estimates that about 3 million Zimbabweans are hungry and threatened by starvation because of the political manipulation of foreign assistance flows and the denial of such assistance to supposed opponents of the regime.

The cause of this colossal fall is not weather, structure, external shocks, adverse trade trends, globalization, or disease. Before about 2000, Zimbabwe had Africa's most balanced economy. It also had the strongest human resource base per capita. Yet this strong, stable, well-run nation in a few short years became Africa's nightmare.

The cause was avarice and ambition. President Robert Gabriel Mugabe of Zimbabwe has always been an authoritarian ruler, albeit an elected one. But in the mid-1990s he began to turn against his own people as they seemed to seek greater freedom of expression and greater control over their own destiny. After he decided in 1998 on his own to dispatch 11,000 Zimbabwean troops to assist the decaying regime of President Laurent Kabila in the Congo, foreign exchange became increasingly scarce and shortages began appearing in the hitherto prosperous shopping centers of Zimbabwe. So did the scale of corruption, for Mugabe made the nation pay for the fuel and other supplies (and the wages) of his troops in the Congo while pocketing himself the payments made by Kabila in the form of a license to take copper, cadmium, and diamonds out of the Congo. Mugabe and his second wife constructed a number of large mansions (so-called palaces), he gave the contract for a new airport terminal to a nephew, and he began more and more brazenly to arrogate to himself and his cronies the remaining spoils of his once proud and stable country.[5]

In 2000, Zimbabweans voted against Mugabe in a referendum. He had never lost an election and reacted with profound hostility to the loss by rigging Zimbabwe's next three parliamentary and presidential elections and, more decisively, by attacking the very basis of his nation's economic underpinnings. He scapegoated white farmers and, in time, forced the backbone of agricultural commerce to flee. Those farmers were also the employers of 400,000 Africans. So jobs were destroyed along with the financial basis of the country's primary industry. But Mugabe and his cronies continued to profit from exchange rate manipulations and arbitrage, by skimming public works contracts, and by raiding the public till. Poverty levels and human insecurity grew inexorably.

Nowhere today are leadership failure and the denial of economic and political opportunity to citizens more evident than in Zimbabwe. Kenya and Nigeria (and Gabon) may have suffered and may continue to suffer as acutely in their different ways as Zaire under Mobutu Sese Seko's benighted rule, but Zimbabwe has fallen the farthest in the fastest time, from a strong, prosperous, internally peaceful state to a nearly failed, impoverished, divided, despairing entity. Mugabe has destroyed Zimbabwe almost entirely by himself. The economy and local terms of trade did not turn sour suddenly, as they sometimes do in the smaller and more economically fragile African states. Zimbabwe's agricultural production was strong, its mining and manufacturing were vibrant, its civil service was competent, its opposition parties were dormant, and it was largely free of internal tensions before Mugabe decided to eviscerate challengers to his power and eliminate those who questioned his right to appropriate the state's wealth as his own. There were precipitating factors—the single-minded decision to send troops into the Congo and thus bankrupt his own country; the increasing scale of his family's corruption; a challenge from aggrieved alleged war veterans; the victimization of commercial farmers; the unanticipated loss of a referendum; and the unexpected effrontery of a serious challenge to his reign by a new class of serious and noncorrupt political opponents.

There was a crisis of legitimacy. Mugabe decided to compel compliance rather than finding more locally and generally acceptable methods to maintain his power and his status as a founding leader. Nor did other African leaders, not even the neighboring hegemon, rise to the challenge posed by Mugabe's defiance of norms and promises. Neither the creation of the New Economic Partnership for Africa's Development nor the establishment of the African Union, with its strictures against misrule, has curbed or is likely to curb Mugabe's excesses.

The chaos in Liberia and Sierra Leone in the 1990s was a direct result of similar leadership misadventures. So were and are the wars in Angola, the Congo, Sudan, and even little Burundi. In each case, as in Zimbabwe, it is possible painstakingly to trace the direct linkages between leadership failure and the intensification of poverty and insecurity. State failure, moreover, depends almost entirely on human agency.[6]

Fortunately, there are positive examples of leadership for good in Africa: In Botswana, Seretse Khama (president from 1966 to 1980) set a clear tone that differentiated his and Botswana's model from the examples of all of his neighbors. The people of the then-poor and ill-served country had to be served well. Incompetence, corruption, and self-dealing were eschewed both by fiat and by example. Khama personally set an example of modesty and nonostentatiousness. He also dealt fairly with his colleagues and opponents, and he provided a consistent, uplifting vision that his fellow citizens could embrace. When the diamond bonanza arrived, Botswana was able to manage it well, and the GDP of the nation-state gradually improved from very poor to modestly rich.

Khama's successors—Ketumile Masire and Festus Mogae—embodied and strengthened the leadership value system that Khama had initiated and perfected. When Mogae, for example, became the third president of Botswana, he was its long-serving minister of finance. In that capacity, acting within the nascent political culture established by Khama and deepened by President Ketumile Masire, he was particularly rigid in compelling politicians—especially members of his country's cabinet—to pay personal debts owed to government agencies.[7] Indeed, his ministry insisted on foreclosure actions against members of his own political party for the reimbursement of outstanding loans. Mogae followed the precepts of Botswana's first presidents in demanding zero tolerance for politically prominent borrowers (and those who took bribes, peculated, or traded influence for perquisites). His and theirs provide a rare African example.

Absent determined visionary leaders such as Nelson Mandela, Mogae, and Senegal's Abdoulaye Wade, and absent a tradition of good governance motivated by vigorous leadership, it often proves difficult for poor, challenged states to deliver political goods in an effective, timely, evenhanded, and successful fashion. They might be able to offer order, but without the openness and tolerance that ensures most (if not all) citizens equal access to service, power, roads, communications, health services, schools, and so on. Poverty is as likely as growth, in such circumstances.

Additionally, Africa lacks a "practical ethic of the public service."[8] Elites have generally failed in persistent practice to demonstrate enthusiasm for the public service ethic, and sub-Saharan Africa appears to lack a tradition of reverence and responsibility for the public domain. There is little culture of "general interest"—another way of expressing the same proposition. At the very least, it may be safe to assert that across four decades, leaders (and therefore followers) have honored the norm of general interest and the ethic of public service more in the breach than in performance. Botswana and Mauritius have been stellar exceptions to that generalization; other nations, possibly including South Africa, may also be endorsers of the norm and the ethic.

The challenge for sub-Saharan Africa is to expand or develop an ethos of good governance and good leadership that can rapidly crowd out the self-interested preferences of venal leaders and replace avarice with a high order of performance. Because this ethos has long been present in Botswana, from one president to the next, and is now mostly present in South Africa and several other critically important African countries, there are no structural or political reasons why the observance of such norms cannot be disseminated and embraced throughout the continent. The demand exists. The supply can be encouraged. Unless leaders begin to satisfy the urge for more accomplished, less self-serving leadership, emphasize the delivery of services and political goods, and learn positive lessons from some of their colleagues in Africa and Asia, then the economic uplift and poverty eradication that sub-Saharan Africa desperately needs will be impossible to achieve and civil conflict will be a recurring phenomenon.

Mugabe, often compared to Cambodia's Pol Pot, has become the poster child of African leadership gone impossibly bad. Mogae, in great contrast, is the inheritor and continuer of Khama's ethic of leadership. Most of the men who lead the nation-states of sub-Saharan Africa—poor and rich, large and small—struggle to achieve the supremacy of a Mugabe without losing their democratic legitimacy and pretensions. How to encourage more citizen-regarding leadership is a decisive question for most of sub-Saharan Africa, and therefore for those who want to assist Africa's assault on poverty, underdevelopment, civil war, and medical disaster.

Notes

1. In a 2002 survey by Afrobarometer, respondents strongly equated democracy with civil liberties and freedom of speech. Fifteen percent of the respondents linked democracy directly with "government by the people." Answers to other questions in the same survey indicated that support for democracy in Africa was widespread, with corruption perceived as a prevalent menace. See Afrobarometer, "Afrobarometer Briefing Paper 1," 2002.

2. See J. Roland Pennock, "Political Development, Political Systems, and Political Goods," *World Politics* 18 (1966): 420–26.

3. These paragraphs draw on a discussion in Robert I. Rotberg, *When States Fail: Causes and Consequences* (Princeton University Press, 2004), 3–4.

4. Todd Moss, "After Mugabe, Zimbabwe Will Need Post-Conflict Response," *Center for Global Development Notes,* December 2005, 2; Michael Clemens and Todd Moss, "Costs and Causes of Zimbabwe's Crisis," *Center for Global Development Notes,* July 2005. Also see "Zimbabweans Have Shortest Lives," BBC News, April 8, 2006. In 1992, life expectancy was fifty-six years. By 2002, it had fallen to thirty-nine years. Also, in 2002, infant mortality rates were at 79 per 1,000 life births (World Bank, *World Development Indicators* [Washington, 2002]).

5. See Robert I. Rotberg, "Africa's Mess, Mugabe's Mayhem," *Foreign Affairs* (September/October 2000): 47–61.

6. See René Lemarchand, "The Democratic Republic of the Congo: From Failure to Potential Reconstruction," in *State Failure and State Weakness in a Time of Terror,* ed. Robert I. Rotberg (Brookings, 2003), 29–70; and William Reno, "Sierra Leone: Warfare in a Post-State Society," in *State Failure,* ed. Rotberg, 71–100.

7. John Holm, "Curbing Corruption through Democratic Accountability: Lessons from Botswana," in *Corruption and Development in Africa,* ed. Kempe Ronald Hope and Bornwell C. Chikulo (New York: Palgrave Macmillan, 2000), 293.

8. J. P. Olivier de Sardan, "A Moral Economy of Corruption in Africa," *Journal of Modern African Studies* 37, no. 1 (1999): 25–52; the citation here is on p. 29.

9

Operating in Insecure Environments

JANE NELSON

The world must advance the causes of security, development and human rights together, otherwise none will succeed. Humanity will not enjoy security without development, it will not enjoy development without security, and it will not enjoy either without respect for human rights. . . . The world needs strong and capable States, effective partnerships with civil society and the private sector, and agile and effective regional and global inter-governmental institutions to mobilize and coordinate collective action.

—United Nations, *In Larger Freedom:*
Towards Development, Security and Human Rights for All[1]

CONDITIONS OF SEVERE political, economic, and physical insecurity, often underpinned by weak governance and high levels of poverty and inequality, continue to blight the lives of millions of people around the world. The poor are particularly vulnerable to the ravages and costs of conflict, natural and economic disasters, repression, corruption, market distortions and externalities, weak legal and regulatory frameworks, and inadequate public institutions.[2]

Yet operating in insecure environments is not only a challenge for low-income households and communities. It is increasingly a challenge for donor agencies; for companies, including both indigenous enterprises and foreign

128

investors; and for nongovernmental organizations (NGOs), including both major humanitarian agencies and local community-based groups.

These different types of organizations operate in insecure environments for a wide variety of reasons—from humanitarian relief, to peace building and development, to the profit motivations of business, such as developing new markets or sourcing raw materials and manufactured products.

The ability of these different organizations to influence conditions in insecure environments for good or bad also varies widely. Such influence depends on factors such as their motivations and purpose; their size; their operating principles, standards, and practices; their flexibility to adapt or shut down operations; their sources of legitimacy and funding; the level and nature of the governance failures they face; and the dynamic interaction between them and other actors, both local and external.

Even within the private sector, there will be obvious differences between industries. Large "footprint" companies—such as energy, mining, agribusiness, infrastructure, and heavy manufacturing, for example—have markedly different risks, responsibilities, and capabilities compared with companies operating in professional and financial services, tourism, or the marketing and distribution of consumer goods. Likewise, operational or service delivery NGOs will differ from advocacy NGOs, and donor agencies with peacekeeping or peace-building mandates from those with an economic development or human rights mandate—although there are increasing overlaps among these different approaches, and a number of NGOs and donors address the full spectrum of mandates.

Despite their differences, donor agencies, companies, and NGOs all face a similar set of broad challenges and opportunities if they aim to operate in insecure environments in a manner that is not only responsible and accountable but also progressive.

This chapter focuses on these broad challenges and opportunities. It reviews current trends; profiles some good practices, especially in the area of collective action; and makes recommendations to organizations operating in such environments.

There is clearly no one-size-fits-all solution for either analyzing or implementing the most appropriate and effective approaches. This is especially the case given the markedly different political, economic, cultural, and environmental conditions and traditions in various insecure environments, in addition to the organizational differences briefly outlined above.

In particular, the level and type of governance gaps and failures in any particular situation will have a major influence on determining the most appropriate and effective response from companies and NGOs—be they indigenous or foreign, public or private. It goes without saying that insecurity due to governments that are authoritarian, repressive, and corrupt will usually be more difficult to address than situations where governments simply lack the institutional and administrative capacity to ensure the security of their citizens. This is not to suggest that the latter situations are easy to resolve, but they are usually more amenable to engagement and support from other actors.

There will also be obvious differences in approach based on:

—*the source or underlying cause of insecurity,* for example, preventing or responding to natural disaster versus conflict, or to conflict driven by ideology or identity issues versus conflict driven by access to economic and natural resources;

—*the extent or severity of insecurity,* for example, a situation where thousands of people are dying or have been killed versus one where people's quality of life and longevity is seriously undermined but not threatened in large numbers, or a situation where insecurity is a localized problem versus one where it is a national or regional challenge; or

—*the stage of the insecurity,* for example, situations prone to conflict, natural disaster, or economic crisis call for *prevention strategies,* and those undergoing such situations need *crisis management strategies,* while those recovering from calamity offer opportunities for *recovery, reconciliation, and reconstruction efforts.* These different strategies are illustrated in figure 9-1.

Notwithstanding all these situational and contextual differences, any organization aiming to act in a responsible, accountable, and progressive manner in an environment that is prone to insecurity, facing insecurity, or recovering from insecurity needs to address the following eight interrelated management challenges and opportunities:

—Do no harm.

—Protect its own employees and assets.

—Extend emergency planning and response strategies to host communities.

—Invest in local socioeconomic development and community resilience.

—Build the local capacity of civil society organizations, community-based initiatives, and the media.

—Focus on high-risk and high-potential population groups—youth, women, indigenous peoples, ethnic and religious minorities.

—Support direct efforts to tackle weak governance and inadequate public institutions.

—Engage in policy dialogue to create the enabling conditions for peace and prosperity.

Figure 9-1. Strategies for Operating in Different Stages of Insecurity

1. Ongoing and systematic development and peace building focused on:
   - A framework for good governance
   - An open and vibrant civil society and media
   - An inclusive process of wealth creation
   - Tolerance of ethnic and religious diversity
   - Investment in human and social capital and community capacity
   - Youth development and enterprise
2. Risk management and preparedness:
   - Implement human rights, anticorruption, and environmental policies
   - Undertake risk and conflict impact assessments
   - Systematic stakeholder engagement
3. Where necessary, preventative diplomacy, deployment, and disarmament to tackle specific conflict triggers and high-risk situations.

Prevention and development strategies

Potential insecurity

Postinsecurity

Existing insecurity

Recovery, reconciliation, and reconstruction strategies	Crisis management and relief strategies
1. Jump-start the economy via new investment and financing arrangements 2. Reestablish the framework of governance and undertake institutional reforms 3. Repair physical infrastructure 4. Rebuild social and human capital 5. Undertake de-mining and disarmament activities 6. Demobilize and retrain ex-combatants 7. Target support at most affected communities, displaced populations, and vulnerable groups	1. Emergency humanitarian relief efforts, using local partners and supplies where possible 2. Security arrangements that respect human rights 3. Aim for neutrality in conflict zones 4. Support peace negotiations 5. Ongoing efforts at long-term development projects

Source: Adapted from Jane Nelson, *The Business of Peace: The Private Sector as a Partner in Conflict Prevention and Resolution* (New York and London: International Alert, Council on Economic Priorities and International Business Leaders Forum, 2000).

Before briefly reviewing each of these areas, it is important to emphasize the limitations of private sector and nongovernmental action. Though companies, business associations, and civil society organizations can support and influence government action, their activities cannot, and should not, be viewed as a substitute for good governance and effective public institutions at the local, national, regional, and global levels. Preventing and resolving severe insecurity must remain first and foremost the fundamental responsibility of nation-states.

Businesses and NGOs have a role to play, however, in the way they manage their own operations to avoid contributing directly to insecurity, the way they manage risks and crises created by situations of conflict and often forms of insecurity, and the way they proactively work with other stakeholders to add value in resolving existing insecurity or preventing future insecurity.

Although the focus of this chapter is on legally established companies and NGOs with the intent to "do no harm," it is important to recognize that large numbers of commercial enterprises and nonprofit organizations directly and intentionally create, exacerbate, and benefit from situations of poverty, conflict, and insecurity. International criminal and terrorist networks, drug trafficking, money laundering, corruption, illicit natural resource exploitation, and the illegal trade in arms are obvious and often interconnected examples that have benefited greatly from the increased freedom of movement of people, information, and money. Often operating illegally or through complex ownership structures and supply chains, such actors are increasingly difficult to control in today's global economy. In certain cases, legal corporations unwittingly become part of their supply chains, as has been the case with "conflict diamonds" and other commodities that are difficult to trace. The need for more cooperative approaches to limit the reach and impact of such "uncivil society" is enormous, but not the primary focus of this chapter.

Do No Harm

A first priority for any private sector or NGO organization operating in an insecure environment is to establish policies and practices that aim to ensure that the organization is not itself a direct cause of insecurity—that its operations do not exacerbate existing conditions of insecurity or create new conditions of insecurity.

At a minimum, companies and NGOs should aim to be compliant with national regulations and applicable international laws, norms, and standards.

They should aim beyond basic compliance, however, to identify and minimize any risks and negative effects of their operations. This is difficult to do in the best of times, but especially so in situations characterized by high levels of insecurity or humanitarian crisis, be these human-made emergencies or the result of natural disaster.

Efforts to secure the safety of an organization's own employees and assets, for example, can result in the use of public or private security forces that intentionally or unintentionally violate the human rights of other citizens. Externally supported humanitarian efforts can sometimes enable rather than sanction the protagonists of an internal civil conflict. Well-intentioned efforts to deliver food and other essential products and services can "crowd out" and even destroy local farmers and businesses, especially small firms and microenterprises, making it even more difficult for communities to achieve longer-term recovery and security. And there are numerous examples of well-resourced foreign donors, NGOs, and investors undermining the long-term capacity and sustainability of local organizations by hiring away their best staff and causing an escalation in the prices of local property and other resources.

Challenges for Humanitarian Agencies

Even the most public-service-oriented NGOs and donors face challenges in terms of "doing no harm" when operating in insecure environments. As the International Federation of Red Cross and Red Crescent Societies has noted, "There is still an assumption in many countries that disaster relief is essentially 'charitable' work and therefore anything that is done in the name of helping disaster victims is acceptable. However, this is far from the truth. . . . The immediacy of disaster relief can often lead NGOs unwittingly to put pressure on themselves, pressure that leads to short-sighted and inappropriate work. Programmes which rely on foreign imports or expertise, projects which pay little attention to local custom and culture, and activities which accept the easy and high media profile tasks of relief but leave for others the less appealing and more difficult ones of disaster preparedness and long-term rehabilitation."[3]

Even for NGOs and donors operating in nonemergency situations and focused on longer-term development efforts, there is a challenge to be genuinely demand driven and responsive to local needs, capacities, and constraints, rather than being driven solely by the organization's own views on what will work or the interests of its funders and other stakeholders back home.

Challenges for the Private Sector

During the past decade, there has been an increase in understanding the links between insecurity, conflict, and economic factors, especially but not only access to natural resources and major infrastructure projects. This has led to a growing recognition that large companies, including some of the world's most respected brands, can also be the cause of, or exacerbate, insecurity— both intentionally and unintentionally.

Although much attention has been focused on the effects of oil, gas, mining, forestry, and infrastructure companies, as well as arms companies and private military enterprises, challenges also exist for other sectors in the effort to "do no harm":

—telecommunications and information technology companies that do not respect user privacy or sell products that could be used by governments to enable increased repression, corruption, or human rights abuses;

—financial institutions that lend to, insure, and invest in major projects, transfer funds across borders, or serve as bankers for the elite in insecure environments;

—pharmaceutical companies that can have an impact on the health and hence economic security of low-income people;

—food, beverage, and agribusiness companies that can either increase or undermine food security and water security, and have a major impact on rural livelihoods;

—manufacturing companies that determine workplace conditions and safety for millions of low-income workers; and

—tourism and travel companies that can either enhance or damage local environments, cultures, and human rights, especially of vulnerable groups such as women and children.

Options for Action

Companies and NGOs have difficult choices to make if they aim to "do no harm" while operating in insecure environments. One of the most difficult choices is whether to withdraw or keep operating. They can elect to shut down their operations, and if they are foreign based, leave the country, or to keep operating and try to do so in a manner that minimizes any harm resulting from the organization's own activities and protects its own people and assets.

It is not unusual for companies from the same industrial sector and even the same country of origin to make different choices, as was the case with those operating in apartheid South Africa, and more recently in Burma and

Sudan. Regardless of the choice made, there is unlikely to be a consensus, even within the organization, let alone more widely on whether withdrawal or "staying in" offers the best option not only for the company but also for the security and economic prospects of citizens in the country in question.

An emerging development that is likely to challenge Western multinationals operating in some of the most difficult and insecure parts of Africa, Asia, Latin America, and the Middle East, from both a competitive and corporate responsibility perspective, is the dramatic increase in major investments that Chinese and other southern multinationals have begun to make in these countries. These new players do not face the same civic activism, reputation threats, and legal challenges in their home countries as their Western counterparts when it comes to accusations of labor, human rights, and environmental abuses. Finding ways to create a "level playing field" in standards and to share good practices will be difficult but increasingly important.

A second major challenge for NGOs and companies that choose to remain operating in insecure environments is whether to limit their responsibility to obeying local laws and regulations in these countries or also adhere to international norms and standards, especially where local laws and regulations are nonexistent, weak, or poorly implemented and sanctioned. As John Ruggie, the UN secretary general's special representative on business and human rights, commented, "The debate about business and human rights would be far less pressing if all Governments faithfully executed their own laws and fulfilled their international obligations."[4]

The challenge is especially great in cases where international norms and standards are not only more demanding but also contradict local laws and regulations—as Yahoo and Google have found in China in seeking to protect the privacy of Internet users and many manufacturing firms have found when it comes to enabling worker participation and the creation of trade unions in countries where such mechanisms are restricted by law.

This is an obvious challenge when it comes to promoting responsible practices and a "do no harm" approach among locally owned companies. Many large national companies have close links to politicians and public officials and do not face the same levels of shareholder and NGO activism as their foreign counterparts. In some cases, they simply lack the capacity and resources to implement responsible standards that will protect the basic rights and security of people affected by their operations.

A third challenge for NGOs and companies is to decide whether they will focus their resources and efforts on implementing their own individual policies, standards, auditing, reporting, and risk and impact assessment practices or will spend time cooperating with others to develop nationwide or industrywide approaches to compliance, risk management, and performance reporting. In the majority of cases, both approaches are being used, but there is a growing emphasis on achieving the harmonization or convergence of human rights, labor, environmental, ethical, and anticorruption standards.

The UN Global Compact, which now has more than 3,000 participating companies, has provided a valuable framework for common corporate principles in these areas. A number of industries, NGO networks, and multistakeholder initiatives have also started to implement common principles and standards. Some of the most notable initiatives are briefly summarized in box 9-1.

Although these initiatives are all "voluntary," with the obvious challenges of monitoring and sanctioning the compliance of signatories, as well as addressing nonjoiners, laggards, and free riders, they do offer useful frameworks for action. In some cases, they are also accounting for large percentages of players in a particular area, which makes them far-reaching even if they are voluntary. The Equator Principles, for example, now cover banks responsible for some 80 percent of all major project finance in developing countries, and participants in the Kimberley Process for diamond certification account for some 99 percent of the global production of rough diamonds. Likewise, the Code of Conduct for the International Red Cross and Red Crescent Movement and NGOs in Disaster Relief has some 350 signatories, including many of the world's major humanitarian agencies, and adherence to a set of Private Voluntary Organization Standards is required for membership in the InterAction network, which constitutes the largest alliance of United States–based international development and humanitarian NGOs.

Principles, codes of conduct, and standards are only part of the equation in ensuring that NGO and business operations "do no harm" in insecure environments. It is also important that organizations develop and implement management tools for identifying their risks, assessing their effects, and measuring and reporting on their performance in such environments—and do so in a manner that goes beyond traditional forms of financial, market, and political risk assessment and financial reporting. Several collective initiatives in this area are worthy of note:

—*The OECD's Risk Awareness Tool for Multinational Enterprises in Weak Governance Zones:* Following an extensive process of consultation with companies, academics, trade unions, and NGOs, the Organization for Economic Cooperation and Development adopted this framework in June 2006 with the aim of helping companies think more systematically about the risks of operating in weak governance zones and how to manage them.

BOX 9-1
Principles, Codes of Conduct, Charters, and Standards for Operating in Insecure Environments

Initiatives focused on NGO accountability and performance standards:

The Code of Conduct for the International Red Cross and Red Crescent Movement and NGOs in Disaster Relief: This code aims to guard standards of behavior rather than provide operational details. It has been signed by more than 350 organizations, and it offers ten Principal Commitments, as well as recommendations to governments and intergovernmental organizations.

InterAction's Private Voluntary Organization Standards: These aim to promote responsible standards in the areas of governance, finance, communications with the U.S. public, management practice, human resources, and programs and public policy. Compliance is a requirement for admission to InterAction.

International Non-Governmental Organizations Accountability Charter: In June 2006, a group of eleven international NGOs signed a groundbreaking charter based on nine core principles and aimed at enhancing accountability and transparency, encouraging stakeholder communication, and improving organizational performance and effectiveness.

Multistakeholder or industry initiatives focused on private sector accountability and performance standards:

The International Finance Corporation's (IFC) Policy and Performance Standards on Social and Environmental Sustainability: Launched in February 2006, this revised policy and set of standards are based on the widest public consultation ever undertaken by the IFC, drawing on input from governments, the private sector, industry associations, intergovernmental organizations, academia, and a wide range of civil society organizations. The standards cover labor rights, human rights, community health and safety, community engagement, indigenous peoples, pollution prevention and abatement, and biodiversity.

(continued)

BOX 9-1
(continued)

The Voluntary Principles on Security and Human Rights: Adopted in 2000, these provide practical guidance to companies on three sets of issues: risk assessment, including the potential for violence; identification of the potential human rights vulnerabilities that firms face as a result of their relationship with public security providers, both military and police, as well as recommendations for how to deal with them; and the same for private security forces. Currently focused on the extractive sector, these principles serve as a potential model for similar initiatives in other sectors, including humanitarian agencies. They have also been integrated into host government agreements and project contracts, illustrating how such initiatives can achieve scale over time through integration into public policy frameworks.

The Equator Principles: Created in 2003 by the IFC and an initial group of ten banks from different countries with the aim of providing a social and environmental screening tool for major project finance deals, the participants in the Equator Principles now account for more than 80 percent of relevant deals in developing countries and include financial institutions from over twenty countries.

The OECD Guidelines on Multinational Enterprises: These guidelines, which were adopted by the Organization for Economic Cooperation and Development in 2000, are supported by a system of national contact points in all thirty-nine countries adhering to the guidelines—government offices to which complaints against specific multinational firms can be made.

Commodity supply chain standards and certification schemes: These include initiatives such as the Kimberley Process for diamonds, the Forest Stewardship Council, the Marine Stewardship Council, and the World Cocoa Initiative.

Manufacturing supply chain standards: Initiatives in this area include the Fair Labor Association, the Ethical Trading Initiative, SA8000, the International Council of Toy Industries' ICTI Care Process, and the Electronic Industry Code of Conduct.

—*The International Alert Conflict-Sensitive Business Practices Tool:* Published in 2005, this tool aims to help companies assess and mitigate both the project and macro-level conflict risks associated with doing business in unstable countries, with an initial focus on the extractive and project finance sectors.

—*Human Rights Impact Assessment Tool:* The International Finance Corporation is working with the International Business Leaders Forum, the Global Compact, companies, and NGOs to develop a tool that will assist companies in identifying, anticipating, and mitigating human rights risks.

—*The Business Leaders Initiative on Human Rights:* Established in 2003 by seven companies, this initiative aims to identify practical ways to apply the aspirations of the Universal Declaration of Human Rights within a business context and to develop evidence-based tools and examples to increase business engagement. After a three-year pilot, the initiative has been extended for a further three years and now includes more than ten global companies from a variety of sectors and countries.

—*The Global Reporting Initiative:* Begun in 1997 and established as an independent entity in 2002, this initiative is a global, multistakeholder effort that has created a set of sustainability reporting guidelines, with sector supplements aimed at increasing both the quantity and quality of reporting on economic, social, and environmental performance by all organizations.

Protecting an Organization's Own Employees and Assets

Beyond aiming to "do no harm" in insecure environments, another priority for any organization is to ensure the security of its own employees, assets, and in some cases local partners.

At the level of the individual organization, this requires implementing many of the same standards and management tools outlined in the previous section. In particular, it requires rigorous and comprehensive risk and impact assessments, as well as emergency planning procedures and the establishment of preparedness guidelines and tools for employees and key business stakeholders. The training of staff and partners is an essential part of this process. The implementation of security mechanisms that protect employees and assets but do not undermine the security, assets, or human rights of nonemployees is another key challenge. The Voluntary Principles on Security and Human Rights, for example, although currently focused on the extractive sector, could be applied to most industries and even to many NGO operations.

Humanitarian agencies in particular are facing increasing challenges in protecting their employees in the face of civil conflicts where belligerents are directly targeting civilians and aid workers. This situation is exacerbated by the fact that even the definition of what constitutes a "secure environment" in complex humanitarian emergencies tends to differ between civilian and military participants and even within the civilian community—emphasizing the need for better communication and the sharing of information between organizations.

Extending Emergency Planning and Response Strategies to Host Communities

A key moral challenge for many NGOs and companies, and in some cases an operational and logistical challenge, is whether and how to extend protection strategies to the local communities where the organization is operating.

The history of complex humanitarian emergencies, whether human-made or natural, is replete with examples of foreign nationals and wealthy local elites being "air-lifted" to safety, while lower-ranking local employees, their families, and communities are left behind. There are no easy answers to this challenge—especially in extreme crises such as the Rwandan genocide and the Asian tsunami. Even in the United States's experience with Hurricane Katrina, the relatively wealthy and well connected were able to escape the immediate danger—often supported by transportation, funding, and other contributions from their employers or from other existing networks and relationships—while the poor and "unconnected" were left behind and are still left behind in rebuilding their lives and livelihoods. Expectations of NGOs and the private sector need to be realistic. In the absence of public sector support, there is only so much that NGOs and companies can do in crisis situations to extend protection and ensure the security of the wider communities where they operate—beyond the "do no harm" strategies outlined above. But they can do something. This is especially the case in the area of emergency planning and preparedness.

Often, lives are lost and assets are destroyed due to a lack of early warning systems, preplanning, clarity, and coordination of the roles and responsibilities of different actors—national versus local or regional government bodies, military versus nonmilitary organizations, public versus private initiatives. Integrated communitywide, industrywide, or regional preparedness strategies and early warning mechanisms can be developed in high-risk environments to address this problem. This requires the establishment of mechanisms for better data collection, analysis, communication, and information sharing between organizations, and plans to ensure better coordination of emergency preparedness and response efforts.

BOX 9-2
The Awareness and Preparedness for Emergencies at the Local Level Process

The Awareness and Preparedness for Emergencies at the Local Level (APELL) process, established by the United Nations Environment Program in cooperation with the chemical industry, aims to help local government and community leaders in developing countries to identify potential hazards in their communities, build local capacity, and implement preparedness measures aimed at responding to and controlling emergencies. Initiated in 1986 in response to a series of chemical and industrial accidents, the APELL process now also includes planning for natural disasters and aims to reduce threats to public health, safety, and the environment. It has been implemented in more than thirty countries and engages hundreds of companies, community groups, and local authorities.

A key strategy used by the UN system in introducing APELL to different countries and communities has been to work through global industry networks such as the International Council of Chemical Associations, the World LP Gas Association, and the International Council of Mining and Metals (ICMM). In November 2005, for example, ICMM and the United Nations Development Program jointly launched a toolkit to help the mining industry work more effectively with local communities in developing and implementing emergency plans. This model of cooperation with industry networks could be replicated in many more sectors and locations around the world, while also helping participating companies to better manage their own social and environmental risks and protect their "social license to operate."

One example of such an approach is the United Nations Environment Program's Awareness and Preparedness for Emergencies at the Local Level process (box 9-2).

Investing in Local Socioeconomic Development and Community Resilience

As summarized in box 9-3, there is a growing recognition of the links between poverty, inequality, insecurity, and conflict. One of the best longer-term investments that companies and NGOs can make in the security and

BOX 9-3
The Links between Poverty, Inequality,
Insecurity, and Conflict

"Poverty increases the risks of conflict through multiple paths. Poor countries are more likely to have weak governments, making it easier for would-be rebels to grab land and vital resources. Resource scarcity can provoke population migrations and displacements that result in conflicts between social groups. Without productive alternatives, young people may turn to violence for material gain, or feel a sense of hopelessness, despair, and rage. Poor farmers who lack basic infrastructure and access to agricultural markets may turn in desperation to narcotics production and trade.... Many slums are controlled by gangs of drug traffickers and traders, who create a vicious cycle of insecurity and poverty. The lack of economically viable options other than criminal activity creates the seedbed of instability—and increases the potential for violence." —United Nations, *Investing in Development: A Practical Plan to Achieve the Millennium Development Goals,* Millennium Project Report to the UN Secretary General (London: Earthscan, 2005), 6.

"The risks of conflict are higher when people live in poverty—where they are marginalized economically, lack access to basic services, and have no means to provide adequately for their families—or where the gap between rich and poor is growing. The risks are also high when people feel they have no political voice or where human rights are denied or violated." —U.K. Department for International Development, "Conflict Reduction and Humanitarian Assistance" (www.dfid.gov.uk/funding/conflict-humanitarian. asp [June 2006]).

"Since the events of 9/11, security has dominated the concerns of decision-makers and policy analysts. Increasingly, security is being framed in narrow terms of the terrorist threat to the developed world. At IISD we argue for a wider understanding of security that encompasses resilience to ecological stresses and disasters, political stability, equitable trade and sustainable livelihoods." —International Institute for Sustainable Development, 2006.

resilience of the countries and communities where they operate is to support more equitable, pro-poor development. They can do this through a wide variety of initiatives that provide low-income communities with access to economic opportunity; affordable and decent health services, education, housing, water and sanitation, energy, credit, insurance, savings and other financial services, or appropriate technology.[5]

Efforts to support local socioeconomic development are likely to be more effective and sustainable if they draw on the core competencies of the companies and NGOs in question. Examples include banks supporting financial services initiatives and information technology companies increasing access to technology, as well as combining both financial and in-kind resources with the sharing of management and technical skills. Such efforts are also likely to be more sustainable if they aim for demand-driven, market-oriented delivery models that achieve either cost-recovery or profitability over time.

There has been a burgeoning of innovation in this area over the past five years driven by a combination of social entrepreneurs; creative corporate social responsibility strategies that include but go far beyond traditional philanthropy; the emergence of a new generation of individual philanthropists who are highly results-oriented and hands-on; greater interest in developing countries on the part of pension funds and socially responsible institutional investors; diaspora communities reinvesting in their home countries; and a massive increase in new types of alliances and partnerships between companies, humanitarian agencies, and donors, both public and private. Growth in the number and reach of microfinance programs, global health partnerships, and business linkage initiatives aimed at supporting small enterprise development are all examples of this trend. Some are led and resourced by large multinational corporations, others by major foundations and development NGOs, and others by intergovernmental or bilateral development agencies. In some cases, the funds are public or philanthropic; in others, they are commercial; and in many, they are a hybrid of these options.

The challenge for donors, companies, and NGOs alike is to understand local needs, constraints, and capacities well enough to be able to determine the most effective combination of public services, traditional charity, "hybrid" social investment models, and commercial business models—and to be able to decide what situations call for a traditional public-goods approach versus a market-driven approach or a combination of both. Working with local partners is usually essential to being able to achieve this degree of insight. Given serious resource constraints in many insecure environments, this in turn often requires investment in building the capacity and resources of such partners, be they private enterprises, local authorities, or community organizations.

Building the Local Capacity of Civil Society Organizations, Community Initiatives, and the Media

There is growing evidence that community-based programs to support development, peace building, and postdisaster or postconflict reconstruction efforts can be highly effective. The World Bank, for example, is finding "that community-driven reconstruction not only makes reconstruction more effective and demand-driven, but also that communities are far better at identifying and prioritizing their reconstruction needs and they do have the necessary capacity if given the resources and management support."[6]

Companies and NGOs operating in insecure environments can play a vital role in helping to build the capacity of local civil society organizations and the media by providing such resources, management support, and opportunities for leadership development. In doing so, they can enable local organizations to be more effective and influential advocates for good governance, human rights, and security. Equally, they can help to improve local operational and service delivery capacity. Both are crucial to addressing the challenges of insecurity and to building longer-term community resilience. In the case of companies, such activities can often be supported through corporate philanthropy budgets or community investment programs, and additional value can be added by harnessing the skills and energies of employees through corporate volunteering initiatives.

Focusing on High-Risk and High-Potential Population Groups: Youth, Women, Indigenous Peoples' Groups, and Ethnic and Religious Minorities

In assessing different options for supporting socioeconomic development and local capacity-building initiatives, companies and NGOs should not only consider what projects will make the best use of their core competencies and available resources, or will align best with their own organizational values and objectives, or are most likely to be sustainable over the longer-term—although these are all important questions to ask. They should also aim to identify projects that will have a high return in terms of helping to improve regional, national, or community-level security and resilience. One obvious way to do this is to target specific population groups that are either especially high risk, in terms of being a likely cause of conflict and instability if they have grievances and no hope, or high potential, in terms of being likely problem solvers and bridge builders in helping to prevent or resolve insecurity and conflict.

Addressing challenges of gender inequity and the lack of empowerment of women is one increasingly well-documented and demonstrated approach. Likewise, there have been many well-studied efforts to support and include economically or politically marginalized groups, which can include indigenous peoples' groups, ethnic and religious minorities, small-scale farmers, and artisanal miners. There are a number of innovative business-NGO-community partnerships emerging in these areas.

The Diamond Development Initiative (DDI) is one such example. Initiated by a coalition of two NGOs, Global Witness and Partnership Africa Canada, and two companies, De Beers and the Rapaport Group, and supported by the World Bank, DDI focuses on understanding and addressing the challenges faced by artisanal diamond mining communities, which are usually extremely poor, marginalized, and prone to conflict situations. The Sierra Leone Peace Diamonds Alliance focuses on similar communities and brings together similar partners, as well as the U.S. Agency for International Development and the U.K. Department for International Development.[7]

International Alert is working with local and foreign companies, business associations, NGOs, and donors in Azerbaijan to develop, among other initiatives, projects to meet the needs of internally displaced people and refugees. In Mindanao, southern Philippines, it has worked with business associations such as the International Business Leaders Forum, Philippine Business for Social Progress, the Muslim Business Forum, and the Mindanao Business Council, together with donors, NGOs, and government and community leaders, to explore common ground and spread economic opportunity among the region's indigenous peoples' groups and Muslim and Christian communities.

One population group that is often a subset of the others—and that offers both high risks and high potential for creating more secure environments—is youth. During the next decade, about 1.2 billion young people will enter the global labor market—the largest entry pool in history—and the vast majority of them will be in developing economies. Experts predict, optimistically, that no more than 300 million new formal sector jobs will be created during the same period. Furthermore, approximately 70 percent of young people in developing countries are not in school past the age of fourteen years. In parts of the Middle East and Africa, more than 50 percent of the population is under the age of twenty-five.

These young people will play a crucial role in the world's ability or failure to meet the challenges of the twenty-first century. Yet, millions of young people have their aspirations and opportunities crushed at an early age by a combination of poverty; poor health; a lack of formal education; a lack of access to economic opportunity and employment; discrimination on the basis of religion, ethnicity, or gender; and the trauma of facing armed conflicts, exploitation, and abuse. Even those who are fortunate enough to receive some education often find it impossible to get jobs in the formal economy, and they face unnecessary obstacles to establishing their own businesses and becoming self-employed. Despite the burgeoning new microenterprise initiatives around the world, for example, almost none of these offer services to youth entrepreneurs.

Failure to provide young people with opportunities to find meaningful work is not only a waste of human potential but can also lead to social alienation, drugs, crime, and violence. In many conflict situations, it is disenfranchised groups of youth, both educated and poorly educated, who are the key source of new recruits for warring factions, terrorist groups, and organized crime.

The crucial importance of youth development, employment, and enterprise is starting to gain the attention it deserves from policymakers, business executives, and civic leaders. The World Bank's *World Development Report 2007* focuses on this subject for the first time in the Bank's history, and box 9-4 provides examples of some innovative alliances between business, NGOs, and governmental agencies aimed at addressing these issues. Yet, increased attention is needed to achieve greater scale and coverage for youth development and enterprise initiatives.

Supporting Direct Efforts to Tackle Weak Governance and Inadequate Institutional Capacity

What, if anything, can companies and NGOs do to address some of the public sector problems that lie at the heart of much insecurity, instability, and poverty? Most notably, what can be done to tackle weak governance on the part of local, regional, and national governments?

In extreme cases, governance failures result in failed states, but there are many less extreme examples where the security of citizens is seriously undermined by weak governance. The World Bank observes that there is substantial overlap between what it defines as low-income countries under stress, and

---

BOX 9-4
Partnerships to Invest in Youth Development, Enterprise, and Employment

The International Youth Foundation, founded in 1990, now operates in some seventy countries supporting programs focused on education, employabil-ity, enterprise development, health, and youth leadership. It works with a wide variety of partners to identify, strengthen, and scale up existing youth programs, including a number of initiatives in conflict-ridden societies rang-ing from the Balkans to the West Bank.

The ImagineNations Group is a global alliance of social entrepreneurs, investors, financial institutions, corporations, and media working together with young people to influence public policy and to catalyze innovative pro-grams in the areas of youth employment and youth entrepreneurship and in media alliances to explode myths about young people and to build bridges between youth across cultures, faiths, politics, gender, age, and language.

Youth Business International supports national programs in about forty countries for youth entrepreneurship, which share a common approach based on public and private start-up funding and mentoring provided by local business people. More than 14,000 young people have been set up in business, and more than 72 percent of them are still in business in their third year, having created an average of three new jobs each.

The Youth Project of Search for Common Ground, established in 1982, under-takes a variety of creative initiatives to help communities and nations in con-flict to move away from adversarial approaches toward collaborative prob-lem solving. It places a strong emphasis on youth work, with activities ranging from local dialogues to nationwide media initiatives.

---

conflict-prone or conflict-affected countries. In particular, the Bank argues that they share many of the same underlying problems of governance and institutional weaknesses, including, "lack of confidence by economic actors; weak state capacity, especially in judicial, financial, fiscal, administrative and regulatory functions; a large informal economy and parallel markets; poor economic policies; widespread unemployment, especially among the young;

lack of skilled labor and low secondary school enrollment; and damaged or obsolete physical capital."[8]

This is an area where collective action by groups of companies and/or NGOs is likely to be more legitimate and effective than if individual nonstate actors try to influence public institutions or governance frameworks on their own. There are three areas where collective action can be especially effective in tackling weak governance.

The first area is tackling corruption. The World Bank estimates that $1 trillion is spent on bribes annually, some 3 percent of global gross domestic product—money that could instead be spent on socioeconomic development and improving human security. A number of encouraging initiatives have been established over the past decade that bring together companies, NGOs, and in some cases governments to improve both public and private sector accountability and transparency as a means to limit corruption. Notable examples include the Extractive Industries Transparency Initiative; the Business Principles for Countering Bribery; and country- or sector-level mechanisms, such as Integrity Pacts and Resource Revenue Management Mechanisms.

The second area is strengthening public institutions and administrative capacity. An efficient and accountable justice system and well-functioning financial, fiscal, and regulatory systems are fundamental to providing the necessary safeguards and public finance to prevent insecurity and enable people to benefit from development. Likewise, affordable and accessible public health and education systems are essential for reducing poverty and insecurity. Many developing country governments lack the administrative capacity and necessary skills and resources to implement and sustain such systems. Companies and NGOs operating in insecure environments can work with each other and with donors and host governments to help fill at least some of these gaps, although care must be taken to manage expectations. In South Africa, for example, the National Business Initiative has supported efforts to strengthen the criminal justice system, improve the quality of management in the public education system, and build local government capacity in regional cities and towns. In Brazil, the American Chamber of Commerce is working with some 3,000 Brazilian and foreign companies and the Brazilian government to support Instituto Qualidade no Ensino, which is addressing management quality issues in approximately 5,000 schools.

The third area is supporting public sector leadership development. Even with the best intentions, many influential public officials in developing countries lack the necessary skills, information, financial resources, and networks to be effective. As the African businessman Mohammed Ibrahim points out,

"Public sector leaders often lack preparation before coming into office, once in office they lack support in terms of access to reliable data, think tanks, and policy advice, and after they leave office they often lack the public stature and support accorded to former statesmen in developed countries, which is an incentive to use their influence while in power to build their assets in illegal as well as legal ways" (comments made at the Brookings-Blum Roundtable, Aspen, August 2–4, 2006). These issues must be addressed to ensure better governance. Foundations, companies, and donors, for example, can support innovative cross-sector and regional leadership development programs. They could also do more to build regional networks of universities, think tanks, and policy institutes, and to help establish effective multisector accountability and transparency mechanisms at both national and regional levels, such as supporting the African Peer Review Mechanism, where political leaders hold each other to account.

Engaging in Policy Dialogue to Create the Enabling Conditions for Peace and Prosperity

A final strategy worth considering for companies and NGOs operating in insecure environments is active and transparent engagement in public policy dialogues. As with efforts to tackle corruption and weak governance, collective initiatives usually offer the best option for achieving the necessary leverage and legitimacy needed to create the broader enabling conditions for longer-term peace and prosperity.

Business and NGO engagement in public policy dialogues aimed at creating these broader enabling conditions can take a variety of forms. Examples include companies' and NGOs' formal participation in the following:

—Regional trade and development dialogues that focus on increasing regional integration, interdependence, and resilience. Most development and conflict resolution projects are established to deal with national rather than cross-border challenges. Yet the regional dimension is often crucial, and effective regional organizations and structures can play a vital role in both preventing and resolving conflict, if given sufficient resources and political priority.

—The development of Poverty Reduction Strategies at the national level.

—Public consultations to improve the overall investment climate in a country, to debate the pros and cons of major infrastructure developments, or to discuss priorities for implementing national plans for the Millennium Development Goals.

—Government task forces to address a particular nation-building challenge such as enterprise development, labor markets and employment, or poor education standards.

—Peace and reconciliation processes, as business-led groups have done in countries as diverse as South Africa, Northern Ireland, Sri Lanka, the Philippines, and Guatemala.

—Public advocacy efforts in donor countries to increase the amount of public funds being allocated to foreign aid or to encourage more equitable trade access for developing countries in Western markets;

—Efforts to improve donor coordination and encourage more holistic, integrated approaches to tackling complex public problems such as health, education, and enterprise development, which are often addressed through numerous unconnected projects and tackled in a vertical rather than cross-functional and integrated manner.

Conclusion

This chapter has aimed to provide a framework for thinking about different ways that companies and NGOs can work with donor and developing country governments and with each other to prevent future insecurity, resolve existing insecurity, or recover from past insecurity.

None of the eight different strategies for engagement is easy to implement. But they are possible. And there is growing evidence that they can have a beneficial impact on both the organizations that implement them and the countries and communities in which these organizations are operating.

Research by the International Business Leaders Forum, International Alert, the UN Global Compact, and others has identified a number of core principles or lessons for effective engagement in efforts to create and sustain secure, resilient, and prosperous societies. The following five principles are useful for all companies and NGOs operating in insecure environments:[9]

The first core principle is strategic commitment. The active leadership of chief executives and boards of directors is essential, backed up by clear policies, incentives, management, and accountability systems to empower local managers. All too often, grand commitments at the top of an organization do not translate into action on the ground due to misaligned incentives or management structures. This is especially important for international organizations with operations in a variety of different insecure environments, and it is relevant for NGOs and donor agencies, as well as corporations.

The second core principle is implementing key performance standards and indicators. Having a clearly defined and sector-relevant set of social, environmental, economic, financial, and human rights performance standards and targets, with a means to measure and monitor progress against these, is equally important—for NGOs and donors as well as companies. Linked to this is the importance of both internal and external reporting and accountability mechanisms, which can range from third-party verification of performance measures to stakeholder-led assurance mechanisms.

The third core principle is comprehensive risk and impact analysis. The implementation of more integrated, enterprisewide risk and impact assessment tools is essential in order to understand the overall "development footprint" of the organization and to identify key risk areas where the organization may be either a target of insecurity or a cause of insecurity.

The fourth core principle is stakeholder engagement. Establishing formal mechanisms for identifying, communicating, consulting, and cooperating with important stakeholders can play an essential role in preparing all parties to be better equipped to deal with emergencies. Such mechanisms can also help to identify and avoid potential problems, and ensure the best possible development outcomes for particular projects or investments.

The fifth core principle is partnership and collective action. The responsibility of any company or NGO is first and foremost for the accountable and progressive management of its own individual operations, in the workplace, along value chains, and in host communities and countries. Yet, when it comes to addressing some of the difficult and complex "public goods" problems associated with weak governance, high levels of poverty, humanitarian crises, and conflict and postconflict situations, collective initiatives within and between different sectors offer some of the best potential for achieving the necessary leverage, scale, sustainability, and legitimacy to make a difference.

During the past decade, we have witnessed fundamental changes in the way donors, companies, and NGOs think about, manage, and account for their impact and responsibilities in developing countries in general, and in insecure environments in particular. Many are shifting from individualistic mind-sets and reactive, issue-driven responses to more collective approaches and proactive, strategic-driven stances. There is a growing recognition that the complex public problems that underpin insecurity and conflict—and that create strategic business risks, and in some cases new market opportunities—cannot be addressed by any one sector or nation operating alone.

Whether these problems involve tackling corruption or climate change, or improving human rights or global health, new approaches are essential—

ones that combine effective public institutions and efficient markets, and that encourage both policy-driven solutions and profit-making opportunities. Such approaches require a combination of individual leadership, organizational effectiveness, and collective action. There are no easy answers and no simple solutions. Yet, there is much to play for. No company, NGO, or donor that has aspirations to operate in insecure environments in a responsible, accountable, and progressive manner can ignore the leadership challenge.

Notes

1. United Nations, "Executive Summary," in *In Larger Freedom: Towards Development, Security and Human Rights for All,* Report of the Secretary General, United Nations General Assembly, A/59/2005 (New York: United Nations, 2005), 1.

2. This chapter draws on several previous documents written by the author and her colleagues: Jane Nelson, *The Business of Peace: The Private Sector as a Partner in Conflict Prevention and Resolution* (New York and London: International Alert, Council on Economic Priorities, and International Business Leaders Forum, 2000); Jane Nelson, Stefanie Held, and Dave Prescott, *Partnering for Success: Business Perspectives on Multistakeholder Partnerships* (Geneva: World Economic Forum, 2005); and Jane Nelson and Jonas Moberg, *Rebuilding Bridges: Opportunities and Challenges for Responsible Private Sector Engagement in Iraq's Reconstruction,* Policy Paper 3 (London: International Business Leaders Forum, 2003).

3. International Federation of Red Cross and Red Crescent Societies, *Code of Conduct for the International Red Cross and Red Crescent Movement and NGOs in Disaster Relief* (www.ifrc.org [June 2006]).

4. United Nations, *Promotion and Protection of Human Rights,* Interim Report of the Special Representative of the Secretary General on the Issue of Human Rights and Transnational Corporations and Other Business Enterprises, Commission on Human Rights, 62nd Session, E/CN.4/2006/97 (New York: United Nations, 2006), 19.

5. United Nations, *Investing in Development: A Practical Plan to Achieve the Millennium Development Goals,* Millennium Project Report to the UN Secretary General (London: Earthscan, 2005), 6.

6. World Bank, *The Role of the World Bank in Conflict and Development: An Evolving Agenda* (Washington, 2003), 29.

7. See U.K. Department for International Development, "Conflict Reduction and Humanitarian Assistance" (www.dfid.gov.uk/funding/conflict-humanitarian.asp [June 2006]).

8. World Bank, *Role of the World Bank in Conflict and Development,* 16.

9. The principles have been adapted from Jane Nelson, "Principles of Corporate Engagement in Conflict Prevention and Resolution," in *The Business of Peace: The Private Sector as a Partner in Conflict Prevention and Resolution.*

10

Breaking the Poverty-Insecurity Nexus: Is Democracy the Answer?

JENNIFER L. WINDSOR

D O POOR PEOPLE have to make a choice between political freedom and freedom from insecurity or want? This question continues to be asked in some academic and policy circles, despite the evidence and lessons learned from the past two decades that all point to the fact that lasting success in all three goals requires an integrated approach.

Although democracy is not a panacea for all ills, it is clearly associated with and essential to achieving lasting success in reducing both poverty and insecurity. The challenge for U.S. policymakers is to further refine strategies, processes, and organizational structures to strengthen the effectiveness of U.S. policies and programs so that they advance all three goals simultaneously.

Defining Terms: The Distortion of Democracy and Its Promotion

The recent debate on trade-offs has partly been spurred by those who have concerns related to the current U.S. administration's motivation and definition of what democracy and its promotion entail. As both academics and serious practitioners have known for years, democracy is about electoral processes and all that is necessary for elections to be fair and meaningful: free association, free speech, and an independent and professional news media. Yet democracy also involves a broader range of vital institutions: an independent judiciary, a meaningful legislative body, and security forces that defer to the authority of elected civilian leaders (and whose purpose is to serve and protect the people). It is also about laws and behavior that reflect democratic values, which means respecting internationally recognized human rights; protecting minority rights in addition to majority rule; tolerating ethnic, religious, linguistic, and political diversity; and ensuring freedom of expression.[1]

Recently, we have seen confusion about—or, more accurately, a caricaturized depiction of—how democracy is promoted by outside actors, including the U.S. government. Democracy promotion is seen variously as (1) only promoting elections, (2) occupying countries to impose a political system on unwilling citizens, or (3) a rhetorical cover for U.S. imperialist tendencies that are really aimed at global dominance, control of oil, or other objectives. The main tools for democracy promotion are diplomacy, the leveraging of aid or trade or memberships to provide incentives for progress toward democracy, and the provision of assistance to support those inside or outside a government who are committed to putting in place or strengthening a democratic system.

Democracy assistance programs typically consist of the provision of training; grant support; facilitation of the flow of information and expertise between democracy activists in and between societies; providing on-site advice and encouragement; visible demonstrations of solidarity; and advocacy on behalf of those working to make their governments more accountable, transparent, representative, and respectful of human rights and the rule of law. The underlying premise of this external assistance is that while democracy can only ultimately be brought about and secured (and continuously resecured) by internal actors in the country, this support, if properly designed and implemented, can make a difference. The role of responsible democracy promotion programs is to facilitate and inform the thinking and strategy development and increase the effectiveness of those within countries working toward political reform, not dictate outcomes or attempt to direct change from the outside.

Addressing Democracy and Poverty: An Integrated Approach to Human Development

For years, scholars and practitioners debated whether the poor had to choose between economic opportunities and political rights, and by extension, whether democratization had to be deferred until national development objectives had been achieved. For years, the promotion of democratic political systems was seen as incompatible with development and the eradication of poverty. Democratic regimes were seen as inferior to authoritarian regimes in creating economic growth and fostering development.

In the past fifteen years, the "development first" approach has been seriously challenged by academics and practitioners alike. Though economic prosperity and performance certainly help the survival of democratic regimes, the number of poor democracies that have been established in the past fifteen years has provided contrary evidence to those who argue that a certain level of development is necessary for democracy to emerge.[2] Nor has the thesis that democratic regimes are worse off in promoting economic growth and development been borne out. A recently released book, *The Democracy Advantage,* provides evidence that over the past forty years, democracies have achieved growth rates equivalent to those of authoritarian regimes.[3] Democracies tend to grow much more consistently than their authoritarian counterparts; they may not match the highest growth rates of some authoritarian regimes, but they also avoid the worst aspects of dictatorships.[4] Nobel Prize winner Amartya Sen has noted that famines have never occurred in democracies, largely due to the information flows and feedback systems that authoritarian systems often lack.[5]

In terms of alleviating poverty, the same study also noted that "citizens of democracy live longer, healthier and more productive lives, on average, than those in autocracies."[6] The interrelationship between democracy and the broader goal of human development is explored and reaffirmed in the United Nations Development Program's (UNDP's) *Human Development Report 2002,* which in its introductory statement boldly declared that "sustained poverty reduction requires equitable growth—but also requires that poor people have political power. And the best way to achieve that in a manner consistent with human development objectives is by building strong and deep forms of democratic governance at all levels of society."[7]

The most beneficial elements of democratic systems in facilitating development include

—accountability of the government to the governed, both through elections (the ultimate accountability mechanism), and through institutions and processes that citizens and civic groups can use to monitor and affect the policymaking process between electoral cycles;

—horizontal accountability—checks and balances within a system, including most especially an independent judicial system;

—opportunities and incentives for public participation;

—the free flow of information within the entire society; and

—the predominance of the rule of law, including a predictable legal system that provides for equal access and opportunity.[8]

The U.S. government, in the evolution of its official foreign assistance policy over the past two decades, has been at the cutting edge of catalyzing the global acceptance of the need to integrate democracy into development. That process began in 1990, and it has continued through the George W. Bush administration.[9] The 2003 U.S. Agency for International Development (USAID) strategy puts it particularly eloquently:

> For the world's poor people, democracy is not a luxury. It is an indispensable instrument of securing accountable government and for ensuring that aid is used effectively. Governance has to be made more responsible, competent, efficient, participatory, open, accountable, lawful, and legitimate. Unless that happens, poorly performing states will not experience the kind of vigorous, sustained development that transforms human development, achieves economic growth and permanently lifts large segments of the population out of poverty.[10]

The Bush administration's decision to link the Millennium Challenge Account to performance on democratic governance is an important contribution that has great potential for fostering such integration. The connection between democracy and development has also been made at the highest levels of U.S. foreign policy, namely, through the U.S. National Security Strategy in 2002 and 2006. Other steps, including the weakening and isolation of USAID (as well as internal decisions within the agency), have been more problematic for continuing the integration of development and democracy.

Choosing a democratic regime does not automatically lead to gains in overall human development. Policy choices still matter—no matter what the regime type—and even systems that have the processes and formal institutions of democracy can be hijacked or undermined by a dominant elite intent on using its political or economic clout to deflect attempts to address poverty eradication and other goals that threaten its status within society. Similarly, entrenched elites can also act—even after a democratic transition has taken place—to limit the processes and institutions by which a democratic system deepens and matures.[11] In doing so, the beneficial aspects of democracy for development—accountability to the governed, equal access to rule of law, equal ability and incentives for popular participation in decision-making—can also be undermined.

The lesson is not to abandon democracy promotion, or defer it to achieve poverty reduction goals. In the end, the transformation of the political, economic, and social structures within a society are inextricably intertwined, and all are necessary to achieve the objectives of sustainable poverty alleviation, broad-based human development, and the creation of strong democracies— all of which should be the goals of U.S. foreign assistance.

Democracy and Insecurity: Is Democracy Part of the Problem or the Solution?

During the past ten years, a variety of governmental and nongovernmental institutions have embarked on a broad exploration of the issues and policy solutions related to insecurity, conflict, and the challenges of fragile or weak states. A number of these analyses have pointed to the importance of democracy as a guarantor of long-term stability and recommend it as an integral part of an approach to prevent or mitigate conflicts and instability.[12]

In the findings from the State Failure Task Force, tasked in the late 1990s to identify factors associated with internal political crises, three variables mattered most in predicting state failure: high levels of infant mortality, a lack of openness to trade, and the absence of a democratic system of government.[13] The benefits of a democratic system are obvious—there are multiple opportunities for those who have become disaffected to participate peacefully through a variety of processes and institutions—including regularly scheduled elections to change leadership and access to an independent judicial system—all of which allow for the channeling of the inevitable differences and conflicts in all societies in a way that avoids the outbreak of violence or the breakdown of a state itself.

The State Failure Task Force also warned that partial democracies— which could be the result of an incomplete transition to democracy or backsliding democracy—were perhaps the most unstable of all. The dangers of democratization were further enumerated by Snyder and Mansfield—who argued that the most likely time for conflict was during a transition to democracy. They cite several cases as evidence that "the turbulent beginning phase of democratization contributed to violence in states with weak political institutions."[14]

The concerns about the instability in a democratization process are real. Putting in place a system of accountability of the government to the governed is ultimately about changing power relations within society. Expanding political representation or shifting political balance between groups can be destabilizing, especially as those who have benefited from the existing power structure, or have something to gain by continuing a conflict, maneuver to maintain or increase their position, and those pushing for more power and access grow impatient and restive.

More recently, the "democratization is dangerous" hypothesis has been challenged by a number of scholars. Some have argued that Snyder and Mansfield's study and research by others do not properly clarify the differences among political transitions, that is, identifying what is and is not democratization, nor do they distinguish between democratically governed elections and conducting a more limited electoral process, which is now a regular practice, even in authoritarian states.[15]

Other critics have performed their own statistical analysis of the relationship between democratization and conflict with somewhat different, and more hopeful, results. If income is controlled as a variable, democratization is not seen as a significant factor associated with either the frequency or the magnitude of conflict. Indeed, those countries that are seen as democratizing have lower rates of conflict than the global level, and the better performance increased particularly if one looked at the most recent data (that is, after the 1990s) for democratizing countries.[16]

Is It Time to Abandon the Freedom Agenda?

The cautions about the connections between partial democracies and insecurity have reappeared in a number of more recent studies about U.S. development strategies and approaches to weak states.[17] These studies have criticized the George W. Bush administration for discrediting democracy promotion. In the context of postconflict environments, some argue that U.S. strategy should be more nuanced and sequenced, including the delay of elections or other potentially polarizing elements of political competition until state institutions are stronger or democratic acculturation has progressed. In the case of a development strategy, the focus and rhetoric should be directed toward encouraging "good governance" to avoid the conflation with the use of military force to impose or force democracy.

The answer is not to drop the goal but to redirect the argument by clarifying definitions, objectives, and approaches. The best route to achieve the key elements of good governance—the rule of law, property rights, accountability, transparency, legitimacy, the free flow of information, and public participation—is through a democratic system of government. No society ever reaches the ideal, but to abandon the pursuit of a democratic society because it is hard to achieve is a mistake.

Similarly, to address postconflict situations, a similar policy recommendation has emerged: The United States and others should be less focused on the accountability of the state to the governed and more focused on establishing a government that is legitimate and "strong," defined as a strong state capacity and good governance. Rule of law initiatives should be less about due process, impartiality, and the independence of a judiciary and more about mechanisms to establish accountability and reconciliation over the past, and a solid system of security to ensure order, including a professional police system. Typically, most recommended strategies include some support for inclusive civil society participation and dialogue at the local level as a nonthreatening way to allow civic engagement without disrupting the building of a state.[18]

One of the concerns about a more limited postconflict strategy is that it may inadvertently foreclose possibilities for the future establishment of a genuine democratic system. The UNDP and others have argued that the period before and after a war is most critical to establishing open, inclusive politics—or installing "new habits of heart." If the end goal is to achieve a democratic system in which the government is ultimately held accountable to the governed, arguably, starting out with an appointed set of leaders—who most often simply reflect the current allocation of economic and political power—may be itself counterproductive because they will have the incentive to set up the political system in a way that protects their own status.[19]

Indeed, delaying elections until some unspecified time in the future may be problematic to the goal of establishing stability itself. The recommended, more sequenced approach may already be in the implementation phase in a number of countries, with mixed results. Though this chapter is not about examining Iraq policy, which is unique in many ways, the fact that early requests for local elections were reportedly summarily dismissed by the Coalition Provisional Authority and the impact that had in the early days in reducing local buy-in to the post-Saddam political transition process raises important questions that should be considered.

The other problem with such an approach is that it assumes that the United States or other outside forces have the power to actually delay or defer elections within a particular society. Elections, for better or worse, have come to be seen as a universal right, and citizens in countries in transition, particularly those moving from an authoritarian system, are eager to have a role in deciding their country's future, no matter the risks. It may be that elections can be deferred in particular cases where the United States, the United

Nations, or other outside forces are occupying a country, but those cases will remain a small subset of the total number of weak or fragile states.

Depoliticizing the Debate

In defending the importance of democracy and its processes pertaining to poverty reduction and insecurity, this chapter does not argue that the Bush administration's policy is above reproach. The fact is that despite the impressive rhetoric and policy statements from this administration, it has not yet put in place adequately calibrated strategies, based on lessons learned, that are aimed at simultaneously addressing the goals of mitigating insecurity, promoting democracy, and reducing poverty within countries.

Moreover, processes for interagency cooperation in developing such strategies to date have been woefully inadequate. Up until the latest announcement of a reformed U.S. foreign assistance process, the administration has tended to simply create new offices and organizations to address development, democracy, and conflict goals, without integrating (and reforming) existing units into the new process.[20] The jury is still out on the latest restructuring and State Department–led unified foreign assistance budgeting process. Most indicate that the process—far from being a truly integrative, thoughtful discussion of how the needs of countries interface with U.S. objectives, and how U.S. resources can be applied to address the most important challenges—still seems to consist of essentially the same old turf battles between regional and functional bureaus, the field and Washington, that have marked internal U.S. government debates on U.S. foreign assistance for decades.

Indeed, there are questions as to whether the new process will further undermine—rather than strengthen—the current U.S. government capacity and ability to promote democracy by encouraging a purely bilateral approach, and an overly mechanistic and self-aggrandizing approach to monitoring and claiming credit for results of assistance interventions.

In debating and clarifying the strategies for reducing poverty and insecurity, the past three decades of history demonstrate that the integration of democracy, democratic governance, and freedom is not just a goal of the current administration; it is a goal that has been integrated into the approach of the international community—as is perhaps best exemplified by UNDP's current strategic goals. Differences on tactics and approaches should not lead to the abandonment of the goal itself, which remains fundamental to human development and human security.

Notes

1. Freedom House includes in its *Survey of Freedom in the World* a broad range of criteria drawn directly from the Universal Declaration of Human Rights, separated into two broad categories, political rights and civil liberties. The category of political rights includes: Are there fair electoral laws, equal campaigning opportunities, fair polling, and honest tabulation of ballots? Are the voters able to endow their freely elected representatives with real power? Is there a significant opposition vote, de facto opposition power, and a realistic possibility for the opposition to increase its support or gain power through elections? Are the people free from domination by the military, foreign powers, totalitarian parties, religious hierarchies, economic oligarchies, or any other powerful group? The civil liberties score is composed of three categories: freedom of expression and belief, association and organizational rights, and the rule of law and human rights. Some of the questions include: Is there an independent judiciary? Does the rule of law prevail in civil and criminal matters? Is the population treated equally under the law? Are police under direct civilian control? Is there protection from political terror, unjustified imprisonment, exile, or torture, whether by groups that support or oppose the system? Is there freedom from war and insurgencies? See the Freedom House website (www.freedomhouse.org) for further information and findings from this survey and others such as Countries at a Crossroads, which are specifically targeted at evaluating government performance in achieving the fundamentals of democratic governance.

2. Larry Diamond, "Economic Development and Democracy Reconsidered," in *Reexamining Democracy: Essays in Honor of Seymour Martin Lipset,* ed. Gary Mark (Thousand Oaks, Calif.: Sage Publications, 1992); Amartya Sen, *Development as Freedom* (New York: Random House, 1999), 149–51; United Nations Development Program, *Human Development Report 2002* (New York, 2002), 56.

3. Morton H. Halperin, Joseph T. Siegle, and Michael M. Weinstein, *The Democratic Advantage: How Democracies Promote Prosperity and Peace* (New York: Routledge, 2005), chap. 2.

4. United Nations Development Program, *Human Development Report 2002,* v.

5. Sen, *Development as Freedom,* 152, 180–86.

6. Halperin, Siegle, and Weinstein, *Democratic Advantage,* 35.

7. United Nations Development Program, *Human Development Report 2002,* v.

8. Halperin, Siegle, and Weinstein, *Democratic Advantage,* 46–48; Sen, *Development as Freedom,* 151–52; United Nations Development Program, *Human Development Report 2002,* 51–61.

9. See Jennifer Windsor, "Democracy and Development: The Evolution of U.S. Foreign Assistance Policy," *Fletcher Forum* 27, no. 2 (2003): 141–50; Jennifer Windsor, "The Mainstreaming of Democracy and Governance in U.S. Development Assistance," in *Foreign Aid and Foreign Policy: Issues for the Next Half Century,* ed. Louis A. Picard, Robert Groelsema, and Terry F. Buss (New York: M. E. Sharpe, forthcoming).

10. U.S. Agency for International Development, "Foreign Aid in the National Interest, January, 2003," January 2003, 42.

11. Adam Przeworski, "What Makes Democracies Endure?" *Journal of Democracy* 7, no. 1 (1996): 39–55; United Nations Development Program, *Human Development Report 2002,* 3; also see Bruce Bueno de Mesquita and Hilton Root, "The Political Roots of Poverty: The Economic Logic of Autocracy," *National Interest,* Summer 2002.

12. See Jeremy M. Weinstein, John Edward Porter, and Stuart E. Eizenstat, *On the Brink: Weak States and U.S. National Security* (Washington: Center for Global Development, 2004); Woodrow Wilson International Center for Scholars, *Preventing the Next Wave of Conflict: Understanding Non-Traditional Threats to Global Stability* (Washington, 2003); and Susan E. Rice, "Poverty Breeds Insecurity," in this volume. Also see U.S. Agency for International Development, *State Failure Task Force Reports,* 1998–2000, USAID Fragile States and Conflict Mitigation Strategies (www.usaid.gov [July 2006]).

13. U.S. Agency for International Development, *State Failure Task Force Report: Phase III Findings, September 30, 2000* (http://globalpolicy.gmu.edu/pitf/SFTF%20Phase%20III%20Report%20Final.pdf [July 2006]).

14. Edward D. Mansfield and Jack Snyder, "Prone to Violence: The Paradox of the Democratic Peace," *National Interest,* Winter 2005–6, 41.

15. For a more recent manifestation of Snyder and Mansfield's argument, see "The Failed States Index: Democracy Now?" at www.foreignpolicy.com. For critics, see Michael McFaul, "Promoting Democracy? Should We? Could We?" paper presented at conference titled Power and Superpower: Global Leadership for the 21st Century, sponsored by the Security and Peace Initiative (http://www.securitypeace.org/pdf/mcfaul.pdf [December 2006]).

16. Halperin, Siegle, and Weinstein, *Democratic Advantage,* 101; also see Carl Gershman, Media Transcript of the Columbia University Saltzman Institute of War and Peace Studies panel discussion on Democratization, Peace, and War (www.columbia.edu/cu/siwps/images/newsletter/paneltranscript2.pdf [July 2006]).

17. Susan E. Rice, "Addressing Weak States: A 21st Century Imperative," paper prepared for conference entitled Power and Superpower: Global Leadership for the 21st Century (www.securitypeace.org/pdf/rice.pdf [July 2006]).

18. Center for Strategic and International Studies, *Play to Win: The Commission on Post-Conflict Reconstruction* (Washington, 2003); Patrick Cronin, "Development in the Shadow of Conflict," in *Security by Other Means: Foreign Assistance, Global Poverty, and American Leadership,* ed. Lael Brainard (Brookings, 2006).

19. United Nations Development Program, *Human Development Report 2002,* chap. 4; Halperin, Siegle, and Weinstein, *Democratic Advantage,* chap. 4.

20. Indeed, I have argued that within USAID, the pursuit of a fragile states initiative has led to the undermining of the capacity of USAID—and the U.S. government—to pursue an effectively integrated strategy between development and democracy, and the administration's fragmented approach to democracy promotion, have been counterproductive to directing democracy resources to the most important needs; see Windsor, "Mainstreaming of Democracy and Governance."

Contributors

Lael Brainard is vice president and director of the Brookings Institution's Global Economy and Development program and holds the Bernard L. Schwartz Chair in International Economics. She served as the deputy assistant to the president for international economic policy and U.S. sherpa to the Group of Eight in the Clinton administration and as an associate professor of applied economics at the Massachusetts Institute of Technology Sloan School of Management. She received master's and doctoral degrees in Economics from Harvard University, where she was a National Science Foundation Fellow.

Derek Chollet is a nonresident fellow at the Brookings Global Economy and Development program. He is also a fellow at the Center for a New American Security and an adjunct associate professor at Georgetown University's Security Studies Program. He previously served as foreign policy adviser to U.S. Senator John Edwards and in the State Department during the Clinton administration.

Colin E. Kahl is an assistant professor in the Security Studies Program at Georgetown University. He has published extensively on the demographic and environmental causes of civil strife in developing countries, including the book *States, Scarcity, and Civil Strife in the Developing World* (2006). He was an international affairs fellow at the Council on Foreign Relations working for the deputy assistant secretary of defense for stability operations from January 2005 to August 2006. He received his B.A. in political science from the University of Michigan in 1993 and his Ph.D. in political science from Columbia University in 2000.

Vinca LaFleur is president of Vinca LaFleur Communications, a Washington-based consultancy that provides professional writing services to U.S. and foreign leaders in government, business, and the nonprofit world. Since 2002, she has also been a visiting fellow in the International Security Program of the Center for Strategic and International Studies. She holds a B.A. from Yale University and an M.A. from the Paul H. Nitze School of Advanced International Studies of Johns Hopkins University.

Edward Miguel is associate professor of economics at the University of California–Berkeley. He received a Ph.D. in both economics and mathematics from Harvard University in 2000, and an S.B. in both economics and mathematics from the Massachusetts Institute of Technology, where he was awarded the Truman Scholarship. His research focus is African economic development, and he has conducted fieldwork in Kenya, Sierra Leone, and Tanzania. His research has been published in leading academic journals, including *Econometrica, Journal of Political Economy, Journal of Politics, Quarterly Journal of Economics,* and *World Politics.* He was awarded the 2005 Kenneth J. Arrow Prize in Health Economics.

Jane Nelson is a senior fellow and director of the Corporate Social Responsibility Initiative at the John F. Kennedy School of Government, Harvard University; a director of the Prince of Wales International Business Leaders Forum; and a nonresident senior fellow at the Brookings Institution.

Anthony Nyong is a senior program specialist, climate change, with the International Development Research Centre (IDRC), Nairobi. Before joining the IDRC, he was an associate professor of geography and the director of the Centre for Environmental Resources and Hazards Research at the University of Jos, Nigeria. He is a coordinating lead author, Africa, for the forthcoming Fourth Assessment Report of the Intergovernmental Panel on Climate Change. He was a START Visiting Scientist at the Stockholm Environment Institute, Oxford, from June to September 2004. He obtained a Ph.D. in geography from McMaster University, Canada.

Susan E. Rice is a senior fellow in the Foreign Policy Studies Program and the Global Economy and Development Program at the Brookings Institution, where her work encompasses a wide range of issues related to U.S. foreign and national security policy. Her long-term research focuses on the national security implications of global poverty and weak states.

Robert I. Rotberg is director of the Program on Intrastate Conflict and Conflict Resolution at the John F. Kennedy School of Government, Harvard University, and president of the World Peace Foundation. Previously, he was professor of political science and history at the Massachusetts Institute of Technology, academic vice president of Tufts University, and president of Lafayette College. He served on U.S. secretary of state Colin Powell's Africa Policy Panel in 2002–3. He is the author of books and articles on African, Asian, and Caribbean politics and history, recently including *When States Fail: Causes and Consequences* (2004), *State Failure and State Weakness in a Time of Terror* (2003), and *Battling Terrorism in the Horn of Africa* (2005).

Marc Sommers is an associate research professor of humanitarian studies at the Fletcher School, Tufts University, and a research fellow at Boston University's African Studies Center. His work has taken him to twenty war-affected countries during the past eighteen years. He has consulted for numerous donor, UN, and nongovernmental agencies. He has received research support from the Ford, Guggenheim, Mellon, and Rotary foundations. He is currently researching youth issues in Rwanda, and terror warfare, child soldiering, and popular culture in Sierra Leone. In 2003 he received the Margaret Mead Award for *Fear in Bongoland: Burundi Refugees in Urban Tanzania* (2001).

Henrik Urdal is senior researcher at the Centre for the Study of Civil War at the International Peace Research Institute, Oslo (PRIO). He has previously worked for the United Nations International Criminal Tribunal for the Former Yugoslavia. His current research focuses on relationships between demographic change, natural resources, and internal armed conflict. He has published articles in a number of journals, including the *European Journal of Population, International Studies Quarterly, Journal of Peace Research,* and *Journal of International Affairs.* He is coeditor of *Demography of Conflict and Violence* (2006) and associate editor of the *Journal of Peace Research.*

Jennifer L. Windsor is the executive director of Freedom House—a nonpartisan, nonprofit organization supporting the expansion of freedom in the world through analysis, advocacy, and action. Freedom House is best known for its annual comparative surveys of the state of political rights, civil liberties, press freedom, and democratic governance in the world. From 1991 to 2001, Windsor worked at the U.S. Agency for International Development (USAID), last serving as the deputy assistant administrator and director of the Center for Democracy and Governance. She is a graduate of the Woodrow Wilson School at Princeton University and Harvard University.

Index

Printed in the United States
133403LV00001B/196-255/A